Bookkeeping

SIMPLIFIED AND SELF-TAUGHT

Bookkeeping

SIMPLIFIED AND SELF-TAUGHT

John Patrick Gorham, M.B.A., Ph.D.

ARCO PUBLISHING, INC.
NEW YORK

Published by Arco Publishing, Inc.
215 Park Avenue South, New York, N.Y. 10003

Library of Congress Cataloging in Publication Data

Gorham, John Patrick.
Bookkeeping simplified and self-taught.

1. Bookkeeping. I. Title.
HF5635.G694 1983 657'.2 82-11316
ISBN 0-668-05456-5 AACR2

Printed in the United States of America

To my wife Maureen and my children,
Maureen, John, Bernadette, Patrick
and Monica

CONTENTS

Bookkeeping

SIMPLIFIED AND SELF-TAUGHT

1

BOOKKEEPING IN THE ACCOUNTING SYSTEM

OBJECTIVES

After completing this chapter, you should be able to:

- Describe the function of bookkeeping as well as the nature and purpose of the information it provides.
- State the purpose of the income statement and the balance sheet.
- Describe the various steps included in the accounting cycle.

THE NATURE OF BOOKKEEPING

Why are you studying bookkeeping? It could be that you are looking to change the type of work you are now doing, or perhaps you want to advance yourself within a company or complete the requirements of your school. Regardless of the reason, bookkeeping is a very practical subject of study and one which will return benefits to you throughout life. In both your personal and business affairs, you will benefit from the order and logic bookkeeping imposes on your financial activities.

The purpose of bookkeeping is to record and summarize financial data. If you have ever created a household budget, prepared an income tax return, or balanced a checkbook, you have engaged in bookkeeping activities. In your attempt to obtain accurate information, you had to correctly record, organize and summarize your financial transactions. If you encountered problems organizing this data, you can well imagine the difficulty of keeping accurate control of the financial affairs of corporations and government agencies.

Every time a business firm buys a typewriter, issues a payroll check, or borrows money from a bank, it is engaging in a business transaction. Even though the firm may have had millions of such transactions during a year, these financial operations must be condensed into a few pages of significant information. The financial system which accomplishes this feat is designed and controlled by accountants. However, it is maintained by bookkeepers who accurately record and summarize the transactions that occur. In order to work effectively within such a system, it is important that you learn how it operates.

One way of visualizing an accounting system is to think of it as being a funnel. Large numbers of individual financial transactions enter the funnel through the top. The recording and summarizing of the data take place within the funnel, and the information that exits at the bottom consists of condensed financial reports (see Figure 1-1).

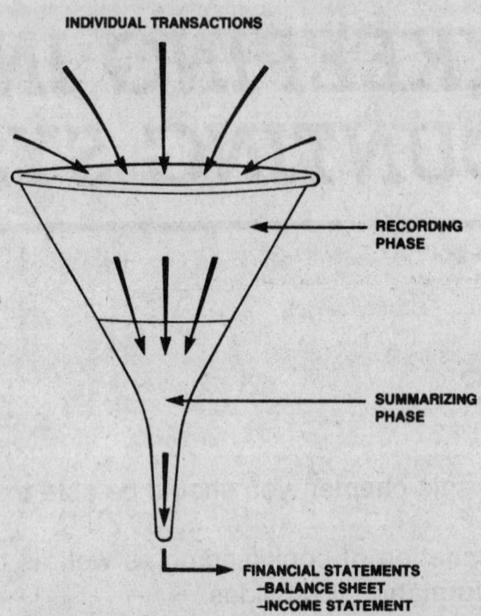

Figure 1-1. The Accounting Funnel

The two most important financial reports "leaving the funnel" are the balance sheet and the income statement. They draw a meaningful picture of the financial condition and profitability of a business. At this time, we will take a brief look at these two reports. The rest of this text will be devoted to analyzing how they are prepared.

A balance sheet shows the financial position of a firm on a specific date. It is expressed in terms of assets, liabilities, and owner's equity.

Edgewood Realty
Balance Sheet
December 31, 19__

ASSETS		LIABILITIES	
Cash	$ 5000—	Accounts Payable	$ 3000—
Accounts Receivable	2000—	Notes Payable	10000—
Prepaid Rent	500—	Total Liabilities	$ 13000—
Office Supplies	1500—		
Office Equipment	5000—	OWNER'S EQUITY	
Building	20000—		
Land	6000—	Joan Wilson, Capital	$ 27000—
Total Assets	40000—	Total Liabilities and Owner's Equity	$ 40000—

The income statement shows if the business achieved its primary objective of earning an acceptable profit over a specific period of time. Many people consider this to be the most important financial statement.

Edgewood Realty
Income Statement
For the Year Ending December 31, 19__

REVENUES		
Commissions Earned		$ 48000 —
Management Fees Earned		12000 —
Total Revenues		$ 60000
OPERATING EXPENSES		
Salaries Expense	$ 34000 —	
Utilities Expense	4000 —	
Office Supplies Expense	5000 —	
Advertising Expense	7000 —	
Total Operating Expenses		50000 —
Net Income		$ 10000 —

These statements are used by managers and other interested parties to evaluate the past performance and present condition of the company. Based on this information, decisions will be made which will influence the future direction of the firm.

It is easy to see, then, that the bookkeeper's task is important. If transactions are not recorded and summarized properly, the errors eventually end up in the financial statements. Only care and attention to detail create accurate financial reports.

THE ACCOUNTING CYCLE

If you wanted to tour the United States by car, you would undoubtedly consult a map and plan your trip in a logical manner. In order to make our "trip" easier, we will use our own "map" to guide us through bookkeeping. Read this section carefully to get an overview of where we will be going in later chapters, but do not be concerned, at this point, if you have difficulty understanding the chart. As you proceed through the text and refer back to the "map," the overall picture will become clear.

The illustrated accounting cycle (see Figure 1-2) is made up of the following steps:

RECORDING PHASE

1. *Business documents are created.* When a company enters into com-

mercial transactions, business documents are produced. They confirm that a transaction has occurred and show the amount of money to be recorded. Some examples of business documents are sales slips, checks, purchase orders and invoices.

2. *Transactions are recorded in the journals.* Each transaction in Step 1 is recorded in a "book of original entry" called a journal. This journal entry provides a chronological record of all transactions and in-

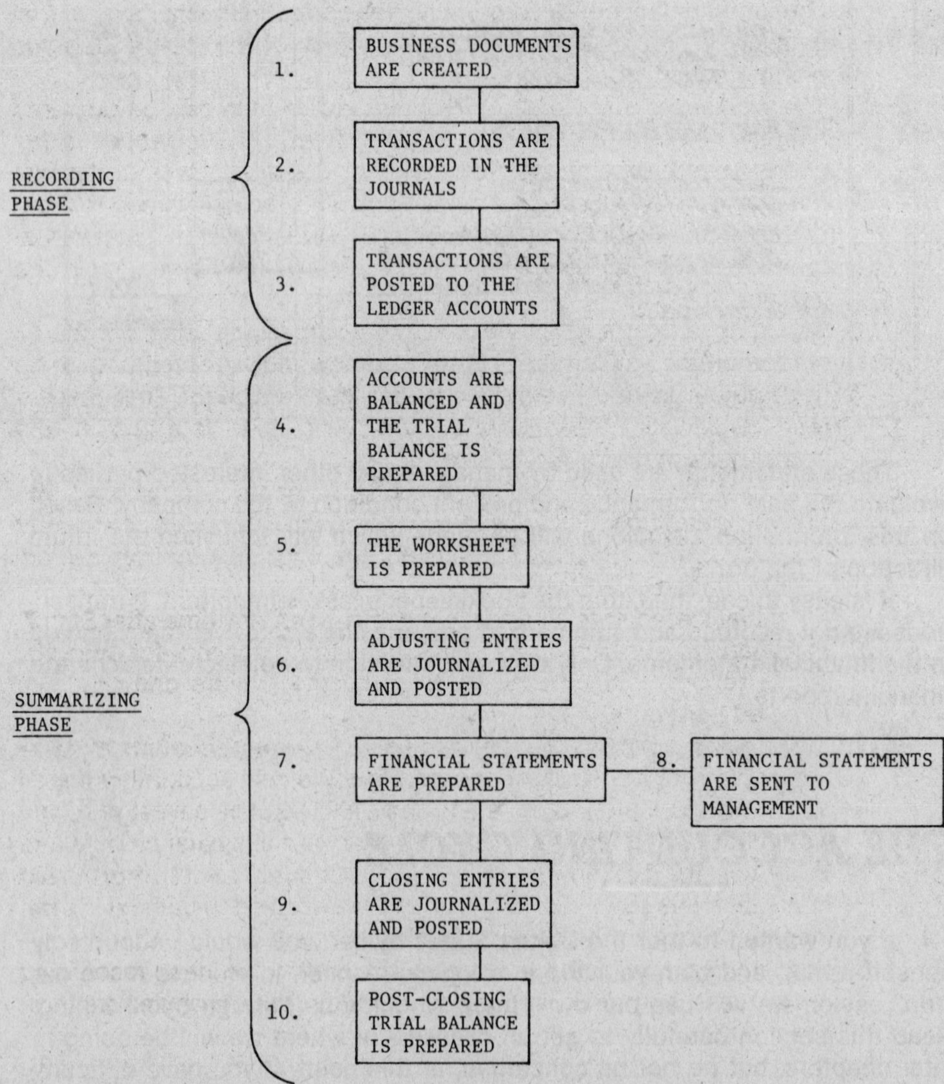

Figure 1-2. Steps in the Accounting Cycle

cludes in one place the amounts involved and the accounts that are affected by the transactions.

3. *Transactions are posted to the ledger accounts.* After the transaction is recorded in a journal, it is necessary to classify and group all similar items. For example, if a company purchased a typewriter for $400 cash, we would have to bring the $400 into the Cash account and reduce our cash balance by that amount. The Cash account is in a "book" of accounts called the *General Ledger.* The process of transferring the increases or decreases from the journal to the proper ledger accounts is called *posting.*

SUMMARIZING PHASE

4. *Accounts are balanced and the trial balance is prepared.* Each account is "balanced" to determine its correct amount, and a trial balance is prepared to check the accuracy of the journalizing and posting activities of Steps 2 and 3.
5. *The worksheet is prepared.* Financial statements can be prepared directly from the account balances. However, a worksheet is frequently used to summarize data and make adjustments to the trial balance developed in Step 4. These adjustments are needed to bring certain account balances up to date. The worksheet is also used to prepare preliminary versions of the income statement and the balance sheet.
6. *Adjusting entries are journalized and posted.* Adjusting entries recorded on the worksheet in Step 5 are now formally recorded in the general journal and posted to the individual accounts. This ensures that the account balances are correct and up-to-date prior to the preparation of financial statements.
7. *Financial statements are prepared.* Statements summarizing the operating and financial activities of the period just ended can now be prepared either from the worksheet (Step 5) or directly from the accounts prepared in Step 6.
8. *Financial statements are sent to management.* Any time after Step 7, the financial statements can be sent to the managers for analysis. These reports will also be received by the owners and other interested parties.
9. *Closing entries are journalized and posted.* Certain accounts must be closed out or given zero balances before the new accounting period starts. For example, if a company had $100,000 of sales last year, you would not want it to start the current year with this balance. A failure to reduce the balance to zero would ultimately result in distorted financial statements. Closing entries are also used to transfer the net income or loss to the owner's Capital account.
10. *Post-closing trial balance is prepared.* Before the new accounting cycle starts, one final check is done to determine if any errors have been made.

2

ACCOUNTS: STORAGE DEVICES FOR DATA

OBJECTIVES

After completing this chapter, you should be able to:

- State the formula for the balance sheet equation.
- Explain why the balance sheet equation must balance at all times.
- Demonstrate your ability to increase and decrease account balances.

THE BALANCE SHEET EQUATION

The balance sheet is one of the most important financial statements and it is divided into three major sections. These are assets, liabilities and owner's equity, defined below:

Assets—Property owned by a business.
Liabilities—Debts owed by the business.
Owner's equity—The owner's investment in the business.

You may have already noticed that the balance sheet was divided into two halves and that the total of the asset side is equal to the total of the liabilities and owner's equity. This is not a coincidence. It illustrates one of the most basic concepts in bookkeeping and serves as the foundation for our entire system of recording transactions. Remember this equation:

ASSETS = LIABILITIES + OWNER'S EQUITY

This equation must always be in balance. If it does not balance, it means an error has been made. At this point, you should be asking yourself, "Why must this equation always be in balance?"

There is a logical explanation which is best illustrated, at this time, with an example on a personal level. If you were to create a list of assets you own, the list might include such items as a house, clothing, an automobile, jewelry, furniture, appliances, and miscellaneous personal property. These possessions are listed along with their value on the left (asset) side of the equation. The right side of the equation describes how you financed these purchases. In order to acquire these assets, you either used your own money or you borrowed the funds from someone, thereby creating a liability. Let's assume that you have $75,000 of assets and that you owe the bank $35,000 (liability), which was borrowed to purchase your house. This means that the bank financed $35,000 of the $75,000 of assets you possess. You must have provided $40,000 yourself, which is your investment (owner's equity) in the assets.

ASSETS = LIABILITIES + OWNER'S EQUITY
$75,000 = $35,000 + $40,000

Therefore, the left side tells us what you own and the right side tells us who supplied these resources. Everything you own has been provided by using either your own resources or those of creditors. You could not have $85,000 of assets, $35,000 of liabilities and $40,000 of owner's equity because the logical question in that situation would be, "Who supplied the extra $10,000 of assets?" This is why the equation must always balance. It is illogical for it to be out of balance.

Account titles are used within each of three sections of the balance sheet so that we can accurately record the effect of a transaction on the assets, liabilities, and owner's equity of the business. Here are some of the most frequently used balance sheet account titles.

ASSETS	=	LIABILITIES	+	OWNER'S EQUITY
Cash		Accounts Payable		Owner's Name, Capital
Accounts Receivable		Notes Payable		(Joan Wilson, Capital)
Prepaid Rent		Unearned Fees		
Office Supplies				
Office Equipment				
Land				
Building				

INCOME STATEMENT ACCOUNTS

We know that the income statement shows us if a business has earned a profit over a period of time. Every business either produces goods or renders a service to the public. In exchange for the product or service, it receives revenue. *A profit occurs when the revenues are larger than the expenses.*

Revenue—The price of the goods sold or services rendered by a business.

In order to produce the goods or services sold, the business must incur expenses.

Expenses—The cost of goods or services used up in the process of obtaining revenue.

It is important for the survival of the business that revenues exceed expenses. When expenses are greater than revenues, it indicates that the company has lost money.

Account titles found in an income statement are easily recognizable.

Revenue Account Title—When a business sells a service, the account title usually describes the service in a word or two, followed by the word *earned* or *revenue*. Some examples are: Commissions Earned, Legal Fees Earned, and Dental Revenue. If it is a product that is sold, instead of a service, the appropriate title is simply Sales.

Expense Account Titles—The first word or two describes the type of expense, followed by the word *expense*. Examples are: Salaries Expense, Rent Expense, and Advertising Expense.

ADDING AND SUBTRACTING IN ACCOUNTS

We have been referring to accounts which have titles. We now need to explore what we can do with these accounts.

Account—Here we record and summarize all increases and decreases to a particular asset, liability, owner's equity, revenue, or expense. For example, increases and decreases in the amount of cash a company has would be shown in the Cash account.

The following analysis of transactions will help to illustrate how accounts are used. Every business transaction (exchange of goods or services) affects parts of the balance sheet equation. In fact, every transaction affects at least two accounts.

Problem: Tom Clark, a recent law school graduate, started his own law practice and engaged in the following transactions:

Transaction 2-1: Placed $5000 in a checking account opened in the name of the business.

Analysis 2-1: The asset Cash increases by $5000. There is no change in his liabilities, but his owner's equity increases by $5000. He financed the increase in assets with his own investment.

	ASSETS	=	LIABILITIES	+	OWNER'S EQUITY
	Cash	=	Accounts Payable	+	Tom Clark, Capital
BEFORE:	0		0		0
TRANSACTION 2-1:	+5,000				+5,000
AFTER:	$5,000	=	0	+	$5,000

Transaction 2-2: Purchased $400 of office supplies and a $600 typewriter on credit.

Analysis 2-2: Office supplies increase by $400, office equipment increases by $600, and, because he incurred a debt, his liabilities increase by $1000.

	ASSETS			= LIABILITIES	+ OWNER'S EQUITY
	Cash	+ Office Supplies	+ Office Equipment	= Accounts Payable	+ Tom Clark, Capital
BEFORE:	$5,000	+ 0	+ 0	= 0	+ $5,000
TRANSACTION 2-2:		400	+ 600	= + 1,000	
AFTER:	$5,000	+ $400	+ $600	= $1,000	+ $5,000

Transaction 2-3: Paid the $1000 debt.

Analysis 2-3: Cash decreases by $1000, but his liabilities also decrease by $1000.

	ASSETS			= LIABILITIES	+ OWNER'S EQUITY
	Cash	+ Office Supplies	+ Office Equipment	= Accounts Payable	+ Tom Clark, Capital
BEFORE:	$5,000	+ $400	+ $600	= $1,000	+ $5,000
TRANSACTION 2-3:	– $1,000			– 1,000	
AFTER:	$4,000	+ $400	+ $600	=	+ $5,000

Notice that after each transaction the equation remained in balance.

The method we have used in this chapter to show increases and decreases is a useful educational tool, but it is not used in practice by bookkeepers. In the next chapter, you will be introduced to the terminology of the bookkeeper—the debit and the credit. They also show increases and decreases in accounts.

PROBLEMS

(Answers on page 107)

1. State the formula for the balance sheet equation.

2. Explain why the balance sheet equation must remain in balance at all times.

3. For each of the following account names, identify the financial statement in which it will be found and the specific section of the statement where it will appear. (*Note:* The first example has been worked out for you.)

ACCOUNT NAME	FINANCIAL STATEMENT	SECTION
Legal Fees Earned	Income Statement	Revenue
Notes Payable		
Accounts Receivable		
Office Supplies		
Rent Expense		
Richard Lent, Capital		
Office Supplies Expense		

4. Arrange the following asset, liability, and owner equity accounts in a balance-sheet-equation form similar to the one used at the end of this chapter. Headings are: Cash; Office Supplies; Furniture; Office Equipment; Accounts Payable; and Richard Lent, Capital. Then show the effect of the following transactions on the accounts by adding and subtracting where necessary. Create a line of totals after each transaction.

a. Richard Lent established a real estate agency by depositing $10,000 at a local bank in the name of the agency.
b. Purchased a desk and chair for the office at a cost of $600.
c. Purchased $200 of office supplies and a $1000 photocopy machine on credit.
d. Paid the $1200 debt.

3

RECORDING TRANSACTIONS IN ACCOUNTS

OBJECTIVES

After completing this chapter, you should be able to:

- Construct a T account.
- Explain the rules for debiting and crediting accounts.
- Use the debit and credit rules to record transactions in T accounts.
- Calculate the current balance in any account.
- Determine the normal balance for any asset, liability or owner's equity account.

In this chapter, we will expand the concept of recording increases and decreases in accounts by studying the double-entry system of recording transactions. The fundamental principles of this system have withstood the test of time. Frater Lucan Pacioli, a Franciscan monk, published his now famous treatise on double-entry bookkeeping in 1494. Five hundred years later, Pacioli's principles remain the foundation of our present system of bookkeeping.

THE T ACCOUNT

The simplest form of account is called the T account because of its similarity to the letter T. The left side of the T is the *debit* side. This is often abbreviated DR., from the Latin word "debere." The right side of the T account is known as the *credit* side and is abbreviated CR., from the Latin word "credere." The name of the account is written on the cross-bar of the T account.

NAME OF ACCOUNT	
DEBIT (DR)	CREDIT (CR)

We must have a T account for every account name in our bookkeeping system. Therefore, if we want to set up accounts for Cash, Office Supplies, Accounts Payable, and Joan Wilson, Capital, they would look like this.

Cash	
DR.	CR.

Office Supplies	
DR.	CR.

Accounts Payable	
DR.	CR.

Joan Wilson, Capital	
DR.	CR.

The number of accounts a business uses depends on the size and complexity of its operations. A small firm may use only twenty, but a large firm may have several thousand accounts. These accounts may be kept in a looseleaf book, called a *ledger*, in which each account is placed on a separate page. Another way to keep the accounts together is to place each account on a card and file all the cards in a card tray, in which case the tray of cards would be the ledger. To simplify this situation, we can say that the ledger is nothing more than a group of accounts.

If we were to take a sample page from a ledger, it would look like the following illustration:

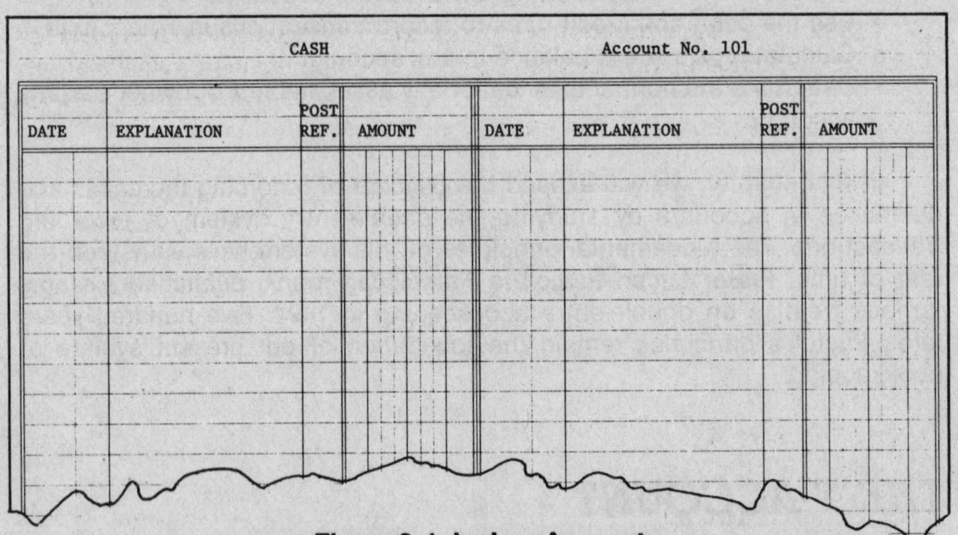

Figure 3-1. Ledger Account

Notice that the basic shape is that of the letter T. The page is divided in the middle by the stem of the T and each side has four identical columns. This structure enables increases to be recorded on one side and decreases on the other. You will not usually see headings printed at the top of each column. They are included here to indicate the type of data to be recorded in the account. The column with Post. Ref. at the top is called the *Posting Reference* or the *Folio* column. It is used to indicate the source of the recorded data. This will be explained in greater detail later (see Chapter 4). The Explanation column is used to record any unusual features of a transaction. In a normal transaction, it would be left blank.

DEBITS AND CREDITS

The words *debit* and *credit* are frequently misunderstood. Many people think that a credit always increases an account balance and that a debit always reduces it. Other people believe that the opposite is always true. We will now see that a credit does show an increase in some situations, but in other situations it decreases the account. This same statement can be made for a debit. Therefore, the only definitions we can make with absolute certainty are:

Debit—The left side of the T account.
Credit—The right side of the T account.

The General Model of Debits and Credits

We will now link what we know about the T account with our knowledge of the basic bookkeeping equation. Every asset, liability, and owner's equity account is represented by a T account. The following general model shows how debits and credits change account balances.

Any Asset Account		=	Any Liability Account		+	Any Owner's Equity Account	
DEBIT INCREASE (+)	CREDIT DECREASE (−)		DEBIT DECREASE (−)	CREDIT INCREASE (+)		DEBIT DECREASE (−)	CREDIT INCREASE (+)

The Asset Model

The model shows us that to increase *any* asset balance we must debit the account, but to decrease the balance we must credit the account.

Transaction 3-1: Roger Hayes purchased $125 of office supplies for his business and paid cash.

Analysis 3-1: Office supplies increases by $125. Since this is an increase in an asset account, Office Supplies must be debited. At the same time, Cash (another asset) decreases by $125 and must be credited. If we assume that he had a $2000 balance in the Cash account, this credit will reduce the balance to $1875.

ASSETS

Office Supplies	
(DR)	(CR)
125	
(+)	

Cash		
Previous	(DR)	(CR)
Balance	2000	125
		(−)

The Liability Model

When we move to the other side of the equation, we see that the effects of debits and credits are reversed. The credit is now used to show an increase and the debit a decrease. A credit to a liability account means that your debts are increasing. When you pay a debt, the liability account is reduced or debited.

Transaction 3-2: Barbara Smith, owner of Overlook Realty, purchased a building and land for a new office. The building cost $160,000 and the land $40,000, for a total cost of $200,000. She paid $50,000 in cash and borrowed $150,000 from a local bank. This bank loan, known as a mortgage, has the property pledged as security against the debt.

Analysis 3-2: Here we see two assets increasing in value. The Building account increases by $160,000 and the Land account increases by $40,000. However, since she paid $50,000 out of her available cash, this asset must decrease (credit) by that amount. We will assume that her previous cash balance was $75,000. After paying out $50,000, she has $25,000 left in her account. She borrowed the remaining $150,000 from the bank, thereby creating a liability. This increase in her liabilities is shown by crediting the account called Mortgage Payable.

	ASSETS						LIABILITIES	
	Cash		Building		Land		Mortgage Payable	
	(DR)	(CR)	(DR)	(CR)	(DR)	(CR)	(DR)	(CR)
Balance	75,000	50,000	160,000		40,000			150,000
		(−)	(+)		(+)			(+)

The Owner's Equity Model

The third type of account in our general model is the owner's equity account, which has the following format.

Any Owner's Equity Account	
DR	CR
DECREASE	INCREASE
(−)	(+)

Actually, this is a bit more complicated than it first appears, but it can be made easy by logical analysis.

We know from our prior work that the owner's equity section represents the owner's investment in the business. The size of this investment can increase or decrease in four different ways:

1. The owner may contribute cash or some other asset to the business. This represents an increase in capital.
2. The owner may withdraw cash or some other asset from the business. This is a decrease in capital.
3. If the business sells a service or product which brings revenue to the firm, the revenue generated increases the owner's capital.
4. If the firm incurs expenses when creating the product or service that is sold to produce revenue, these expenses decrease the owner's capital or investment.

It would appear that we should enter the increases or decreases caused by these four types of transactions in one account—the Capital account.

Roger Hayes, Capital

(DR)	(CR)
DECREASE (−)	INCREASE (+)
(−) Withdrawals of capital	(+) Contributions of capital
(−) Expenses	(+) Revenue

The problem with using only one account to record all of these types of transactions is that it becomes very difficult to identify what our total revenues, expenses, or withdrawals are unless we sift through all of the transactions. It is easier to establish four accounts: one for each type of transaction. However, at year-end, when we want to produce our financial statements, we will need one capital amount in the owner's equity section of the balance sheet. This amount must reflect the increases and decreases caused by revenues, expenses, and withdrawals in the previous year. We will resolve this conflict by establishing four separate accounts for use during the year. Then, at the end of the year, we will bring the final balances in revenue, expense and withdrawal accounts back over to the Capital account, which is our principal owner's equity account.

Owner's Name, Capital

DR	CR
DECREASE	INCREASE
(−)	(+)

Owner's Name, Withdrawals

DR	CR
INCREASE	DECREASE
(+)	(−)

Revenue Accounts

DR	CR
DECREASE	INCREASE
(−)	(+)

Expense Accounts

DR	CR
INCREASE	DECREASE
(+)	(−)

The two types of accounts which decrease capital (withdrawals and expenses) accumulate debit balances during the year. These balances are eventually transferred to the debit of the Capital account, producing a decrease in the owner's investment. Revenue accounts build up credit balances which are then transferred to the credit side of the Capital account. At the end of the accounting period, these credits will help to boost the owner's investment.

You may have noticed that the debits in the withdrawal and expense accounts are labeled "increase," but when these amounts are transferred to the Capital account, they become decreases. The only reason the debit side is labeled "increase" is because it accumulates, or builds up, a debit balance during the year. The "increase" refers specifically to this build-up and not to the ultimate impact in the Capital account.

Transaction 3-3: John Walsh invested $20,000 to establish a dental practice.

Analysis 3-3: The asset Cash increases by $10,000 and is therefore debited. Dr. Walsh's investment in his practice increases to $10,000, which is shown by a credit to the Capital account.

ASSETS
Cash

DR	CR
10,000	
(+)	

OWNER'S EQUITY
John Walsh, Capital

DR	CR
	10,000
	(+)

Transaction 3-4: Completed dental work for a patient and collected $100.

Analysis 3-4: Debit Cash because this asset is increasing. Credit Dental Revenue to show the increase in revenue. The $100 in the Dental Revenue account will appear in the revenue section of the income statement and will eventually increase the credit side of the Capital account.

ASSETS
Cash

	DR	CR
Balance	10,000	
	100	
	(+)	

OWNER'S EQUITY
Dental Revenue

DR	CR
	100
	(+)

Transaction 3-5: Completed dental work and billed the patient $225.

Analysis 3-5: The patient did not pay when the services were rendered, so we cannot debit Cash. Instead, the debit must go to Accounts Receivable, which is also an asset. This account now shows our right to receive $225 from the patient. Although Walsh is not collecting cash for his services, we can still credit the Dental Revenue account because he performed the service and earned the right to receive payment. A revenue account is credited when the service is performed. The receipt of cash plays no role in determining which account we credit.

ASSETS
Accounts Receivable

DR	CR
225	
(+)	

OWNER'S EQUITY
Dental Revenue

DR	CR	
	100	Balance
	(+)	
	225	

Transaction 3-6: At the end of the first month, paid $600 rent on the office.

Analysis 3-6: Credit Cash to reflect the outflow of money. The debit is to Rent Expense. In order to determine when an expense account should be debited, ask yourself, "Has an asset been used up or consumed?" In this situation, John Walsh has used the office space for one month and is now recognizing this fact in his financial records. If he had paid the rent in advance, we would have debited Prepaid Rent (asset) because he had not yet used the asset. At the end of the month, the $600 would have been removed from the asset account and recorded as an expense.

ASSETS
Cash

DR	CR
10,000	600
100	(−)

OWNER'S EQUITY
Rent Expense

DR	CR
600	
(+)	

Transaction 3-7: Purchased $300 of dental supplies on credit.

Analysis 3-7: Debit Dental Supplies, an asset account, for $300. The ledger would also contain a Dental Supplies Expense account, but this would not receive the debit because he has not consumed the asset. At this point, the supplies are stored in his office. After they are used, the $300 will be transferred to the expense account. Accounts Payable is credited because he incurred a liability.

ASSET
Dental Supplies

DR	CR
300	
(+)	

LIABILITY
Accounts Payable

DR	CR
	300
	(+)

Transaction 3-8: Recognized the fact that $300 of dental supplies has been used.

Analysis 3-8: Now that the asset has been completely used, the expense can be debited and the asset account reduced with a credit. Dental Supplies Expense will appear on the income statement along with other expenses. This debit balance in the expense account will eventually be transferred to the debit side of the capital account. The ultimate impact will be a decrease in his investment in the business.

	ASSET Dental Supplies		OWNER'S EQUITY Dental Supplies Expense	
	DR	CR	DR	CR
Balance	300	300	300	
		(−)	(+)	

Transaction 3-9: Withdrew $1,000 to pay personal expenses.

Analysis 3-9: The debit is to the Withdrawal account. This debit balance will be transferred to the debit side of the Capital account at the end of the accounting period. The credit is to the asset withdrawn from the business, in this case Cash. If he had removed a typewriter from the firm, we would have reduced (credited) Office Equipment.

ASSET Cash		OWNER'S EQUITY John Walsh, Withdrawals	
DR	CR	DR	CR
10,000	600	1,000	
100	1,000	(+)	
	(−)		

Did you notice that in each of the preceding transactions we used at least two accounts and that the debits and credits were equal? Did you also observe that our bookkeeping equation (Assets = Liabilities + Owner's Equity) was always in balance? These are some of the prominent features of the double-entry system of bookkeeping.

PARTNER'S EQUITY AND STOCKHOLDERS' EQUITY

In the foregoing illustration we used a single Capital account for the owner of the firm. This will not change significantly if the firm is organized as a partnership. Since a partnership has two or more owners, it is only necessary to set up a Capital account and a Withdrawal account for each partner. If K. Donahue and J. Lee conduct business as a partnership, the owner's equity accounts in the general ledger would be:

K. Donahue, Capital		J. Lee, Capital	
	24,000		13,000

K. Donahue, Withdrawals		J. Lee, Withdrawals	
4,000		3,000	

On the balance sheet, the Owner's Equity section would be identified as Partner's Equity and contain the ending capital balance for each partner.

Partner's Equity		
K. Donahue, Capital	$20,000	
J. Lee, Capital	10,000	
Total Partner's Equity		$30,000

Businesses organized as corporations are somewhat more complicated and will not be discussed in detail here. Corporations frequently have many owners, each of whom has bought shares of stock in the company. Instead of having one Capital and one Withdrawal account for each owner, the company may use only a Common Stock account, a Retained Earnings Account, and a Dividend account.

The Common Stock account represents the stockholders' original investment in the corporation. The balance in the Retained Earnings account represents the increase in value of the stockholders' original investment. It is increased when the company earns a profit and decreased when a loss is incurred and when a dividend is paid to the stockholders.

The Dividend account is very similar to the Withdrawal account in that its balance reflects a distribution of assets to the stockholders and, consequently, a reduction of the owner's investment in the firm. Unlike the Retained Earnings account, which carries a balance from one year to the next, the Dividend account starts each year with a zero balance.

Let us assume that at the end of the year the Steuben Corporation had the following balances:

Common Stock	
	300,000

Retained Earnings	
	60,000

The Stockholders' Equity section of the balance sheet would be reported as follows:

Stockholders' Equity		
Common Stock	$300,000	
Retained Earnings	60,000	
Total Stockholders' Equity		$360,000

BALANCING THE ACCOUNT

Over a period of time, an account will be debited and credited many times. In the series of transactions just completed, the Cash account received two debits and two credits.

Cash	
10,000	600
100	1,000

If we want to know the current balance of the account, we should follow a simple set of procedures.

1. Add the amounts recorded on the debit side and write the total in the Amount column.
2. Do the same on the credit side.
3. Subtract the smaller from the larger total and enter the difference, which is the account balance, in the amount column of the side with the larger total. If the debit total is larger than the credit total, the account has a debit balance. When the credit side is larger, the balance is a credit balance.

Cash			
10,000	600	$10,100	Debits
100	1,000	1,600	Credits
10,100	1,600	$ 8,500	Balance
(Bal.) 8,500			

In this illustration, the total is $10,100 and the sum of the credits is $1600. Since the debit side has the larger total, we know the account has a debit balance. When we subtract the smaller credit total ($1600) from the debit ($10,100), we find a difference of $8500. We now know that the account has a debit balance of $8500. If we were preparing a balance sheet today, this is the amount we would record as our Cash balance.

NORMAL ACCOUNT BALANCES

Each account has what is referred to as a "normal" balance. This is the balance one would logically expect to find if the balance were not zero. We just saw that accounts can have debit or credit balances and that Cash had a debit balance. Rather than attempting to analyze each account individually, we will classify each type of account with its "normal" balance. The normal balance of an account is directly related to the method of increasing the account.

	INCREASE	DECREASE	NORMAL BALANCE
Asset	Debit	Credit	Debit
Liability	Credit	Debit	Credit
Owner's Equity Accounts			
Capital	Credit	Debit	Credit

	INCREASE	DECREASE	NORMAL BALANCE
Revenue	Credit	Debit	Credit
Expense	Debit	Credit	Debit
Withdrawal	Debit	Credit	Debit

The normal balance for an account is the same as the debit or credit needed to increase the account. This is because an account either has a positive value or a zero value. A negative or below-zero value makes no sense when you consider what this means. For an asset such as land, one could reason, "I either have land, which is shown by a debit balance, or I have no land, which means a zero balance, but I cannot have less than no (zero) land. Therefore, I would never expect to find a credit balance in the Land account." This type of reasoning can be applied to each account. Try it. You will find that if a debit is used to show an increase, then it will have a normal debit balance. When a credit increases an account its normal balance will be a credit balance.

PROBLEMS

(Answers on page 108)

1. The ledger of the Hynes Co. contains the following accounts. For each, indicate the type of account it is and show how you would increase and decrease the balance by writing the words "debit" or "credit" in the proper columns. In the last column, indicate the normal balance for the account by writing "debit" or "credit."

ACCOUNT	TYPE OF ACCOUNT	INCREASE	DECREASE	NORMAL BALANCE
Cash	Asset	Debit	Credit	Debit
Accounts Payable				
Interest Expense				
William Hynes, Withdrawals				
Accounts Receivable				
Rental Fees Earned				
Unearned Fees				
William Hynes, Capital				

2. The following accounts are in the ledger of Augustine Realty: Cash; Accounts Receivable; Office Supplies; Office Equipment; Accounts Payable; Robert Augustine, Capital; Robert Augustine, Withdrawals; Commissions Earned; Advertising Expense; Rent Expense; Utilities Expense.

Part I. Create a T account for each of the above and record the following transactions. Use the transaction letters to identify the amounts in the T accounts.

- **a.** Invested $10,000 to establish the business.
- **b.** Purchased office equipment on account, $4,000.
- **c.** Paid $75 for office supplies.
- **d.** Received $2000 commission for selling a house.

e. Paid $125 for an advertisement in the local paper.
f. Billed a customer $3500 for services performed in selling his house.
g. Withdrew $600 cash for personal use.
h. Paid electricity bill, $120.
i. Received $1500 of the $3500 due from customer.
j. Paid $2000 of the $4400 office equipment debt.
k. Paid the rent for the month, $480.

Part II. Determine the final balance in each account.

4

THE GENERAL JOURNAL

OBJECTIVES

After completing this chapter, you should be able to:

- Explain the advantages of recording transactions in a general journal.
- Record transactions in a general journal.
- Post general journal entries to the ledger accounts.
- Prepare a trial balance to test the accuracy of the recording and posting activities.
- Explain various techniques for locating errors that arise in the recording process.

THE NEED FOR A JOURNAL

In the last chapter, we saw that we could record transactions directly in the general ledger accounts. This was done only to acquaint you with the concept of the debit and the credit. You may have already noticed, if you referred back to the accounting cycle flowchart in Chapter 1, that we left out Step 2 in the recording phase. This calls for us to record transactions in the journals before posting to the individual accounts in the ledger.

By using both a journal and a ledger, we obtain certain benefits which are not available when we record transactions directly in the ledger:

1. All the information about a transaction is recorded in one place.
2. The journal allows us to record an explanation of each entry.
3. With the journal, we build a chronological (day-by-day) record of transactions.
4. The detection of errors is made easier.

Businesses frequently use several types of journals, but in this chapter we will look only at the *General Journal*. This is the simplest and most flexible journal.

JOURNALIZING TRANSACTIONS

The term *journalizing* refers to the process of recording transactions in journals. The journal itself is often called the *book of original entry* because this is where we first record transactions. To record transactions in a general journal we must:

1. *Record the date.*
   a. The year is written once on each page, at the top of the Date column.
   b. The month is recorded on the first line only of the Date column, except when the month changes.
   c. The day is written in the Date column on the first line used for each transaction. Remember, the day must be recorded once for each transaction, regardless of the number of transactions.
2. *Record the debit.* Write the title of the account to be debited in the Account Titles and Explanation sections. It is recorded on the same line as the date and is alongside of the left margin. Next, record the amount in the debit column. It is important to remember that debits are always recorded before credits.
3. *Record the credit.* On the next line, the name of the account to be credited is written approximately one inch in from the margin. The amount is then entered in the credit column.
4. *Write the explanation.* A brief explanation of the transaction may be written on the next line. The explanation should consist of only a few words and should start approximately one-half inch from the margin. (In this text, explanations will be given for the first few entries but will thereafter be omitted.)
5. *Skip one line between transactions.* This is done to set each journal entry apart from all others. Do not skip a line *within* a journal entry, only between them.

GENERAL JOURNAL PAGE 7

DATE	ACCOUNT TITLES AND EXPLANATION	POST. REF.	DEBIT	CREDIT
19 May 6	Advertising Expense		140—	
	Cash			140—
	Advertisement in Edgewood News			
6	Office Supplies		300—	
	Office Equipment		500—	
	Accounts Payable			800—
	Purchased from Moore Co. on acct.			
7	Accounts Payable		800—	
	Cash			800—
	Paid amount owed Moore Co.			

POSTING JOURNAL ENTRIES TO ACCOUNTS

So far, we have recorded the transactions in the general journal, but now we must transfer these amounts to the individual accounts, which, as you know, are in the general ledger. This posting is normally done near the end of each day. Every debit in the journal will ultimately become a debit in a ledger account, and every journal credit will become a ledger account credit.

The steps in posting are (refer to General Journal on page 26):

1. Find the account to be debited in the ledger. If your journal entry shows a debit to Advertising Expense, then this is the account you must locate in the ledger.
2. On the debit side of the account write:
   a. the *date* of the entry as recorded in the journal.
   b. the *journal page number* from which the debit is being posted. This is written in the *Posting Reference* (Post Ref.) column. Notice that the letter "J" precedes the page number. This indicates that the amount came from page 7 of the general journal. Later, we will use other special journals, which will be identified by other letters.
   c. the amount to be debited in the Amount column.
3. In the Posting Reference column of the journal, enter the number of the account to which the amount was posted. This provides a cross-reference between the journal and the ledger.
4. Repeat the preceding steps for the credit side of the journal entry.

CREATING THE TRIAL BALANCE

A brief review of the procedures we have studied to this point will help us to appreciate the usefulness of the trial balance. We know that every business transaction entered into by a company causes a general journal entry to be created. We have also seen that in each journal entry the total of the debits equals the total of the credits. Our next procedure was to transfer the debits and credits in the journal to the respective debit and credit columns in the ledger accounts. Logically, if we have made no errors in recording the transaction in the journal and ledger, the total of all the debits in the ledger must be equal to the total of all the credits.

The trial balance is used as a proof of the equality of debit and credit balances in the ledger. It is not, however, used to prove the accuracy of the accounts. For example, if you erroneously debited Accounts Receivable when you should have debited Accounts Payable, the trial balance would still show an equality of debits and credits but two accounts would have incorrect balances. Similarly, if we were to omit recording an entire transaction, the trial balance would not detect the error. *The only proof offered by the trial balance is that there is an equality of debits and credits.*

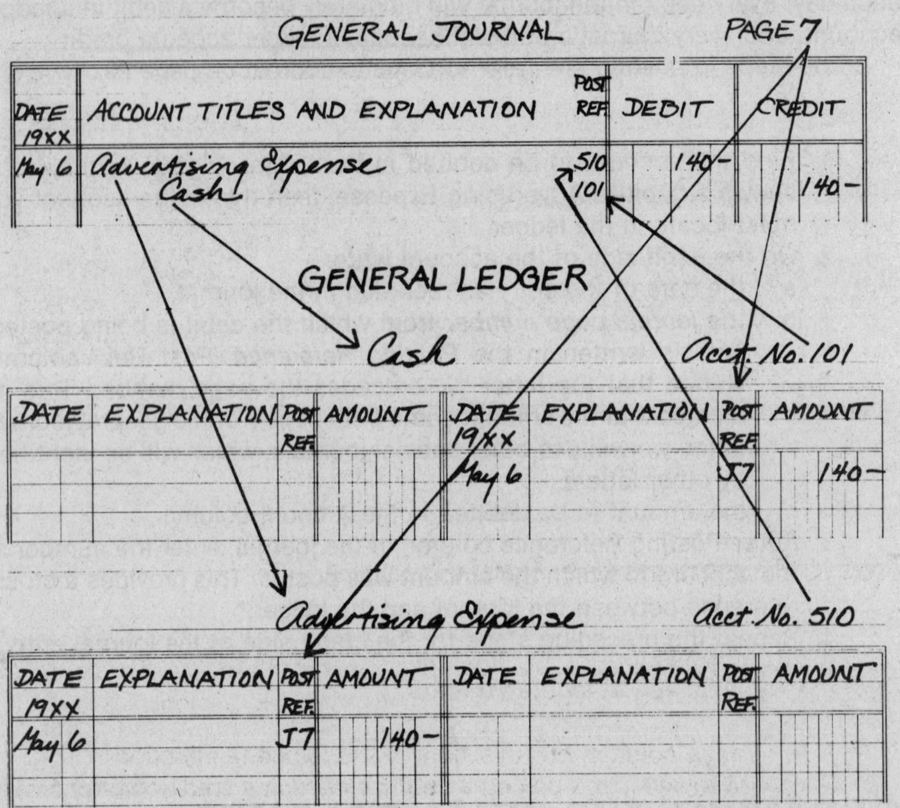

The trial balance is a two-column schedule listing the names and balances of all accounts. (See page 27 for the June 30 trial balance of the Redwood Real Estate Co.)

The steps to follow in preparing a trial balance are:

1. Determine the balance of each ledger account.
2. List each account which has a balance in the trial balance. If an account balance is zero, do not record it.

3. Record debit balances in the left column and credits on the right side.
4. Add each column.
5. Compare the column totals to be sure they are equal.

Redwood Real Estate Co.
Trial Balance
June 30, 19—

	Debits	Credits
Cash	$ 21200 –	
Accounts Receivable	9000 –	
Land	10000 –	
Building	57000 –	
Furniture	6200 –	
Accounts Payable		$ 7700 –
Thomas Reynolds, Capital		95700 –
	$ 103400 –	$ 103400 –

Tracing Errors in the Trial Balance

It is not unusual to find that the column totals are not equal. The following steps will help you to locate the error.

1. Add each column, but this time in the opposite direction.
2. Check to see if you placed a debit balance in a credit column or vice versa.
3. Compare the balances in the ledger accounts with those you recorded on the trial balance.
4. Check your postings from the journal to the ledger.
5. Recompute the balance of each account.

A useful technique, which will sometimes lead you directly to the error, is to find the difference between the column totals.

1. If the difference is $0.01, $0.10, $1.00, $10.00, $100.00 or similar number, the error may be due to faulty addition or subtraction.
2. If the difference between totals is evenly divisible by 9, you may have made a *transposition error*. A transposition error is created when numbers are exchanged in their order as they are being recorded. For example, if the Office Supplies account balance is $984, but you recorded it on the trial balance as $948, the difference, $36, is evenly divisible by 9.
3. If the trial balance difference is divisible by 2, check to see if this number is equal to one of the entries. You may have recorded a debit as a credit or a credit as a debit.

DEMONSTRATION PROBLEM

The following series of transactions will be used to illustrate many of the principles and procedures we have been studying.

Transactions

- **a.** Kathleen O'Brien established O'Brien Decorators and deposited $12,000 in a bank account opened in the name of the business.
- **b.** Purchased $650 of office equipment on account.
- **c.** Purchased $225 of office supplies for cash.
- **d.** Paid rent for the month, $300.
- **e.** Purchased a small truck for $12,000, paying $4000 in cash and issuing a note payable for the balance.
- **f.** Purchased $175 of office supplies on account.
- **g.** Completed a job and received $500 cash.
- **h.** Paid insurance premiums, $600.
- **i.** Paid $650 due on purchase of office equipment.
- **j.** Completed a job and billed client $1000.

General Journal Entries

		1	2
a.	Cash	12000 —	
	Kathleen O'Brien, Capital		12000 —
b.	Office Equipment	650 —	
	Accounts Payable		650 —
c.	Office Supplies	225 —	
	Cash		225 —
d.	Rent Expense	300 —	
	Cash		300 —
e.	Truck	12000 —	
	Cash		4000 —
	Notes Payable		8000 —
f.	Office Supplies	175 —	
	Accounts Payable		175 —
g.	Cash	500 —	
	Fees Earned		500 —
h.	Prepaid Insurance	600 —	
	Cash		600 —
i	Accounts Payable	650 —	
	Cash		650 —
j.	Accounts Receivable	1000 —	
	Fees Earned		1000 —

General Ledger Accounts

Cash

	Debit		Credit
(a)	12000—	(c)	225—
(g)	500—	(d)	300—
		(e)	4000—
		(h)	600—
		(i)	650—
	12500—		5775—
(BAL)	6725—		

Accounts Receivable

	Debit		Credit
(j)	1000—		

Prepaid Insurance

	Debit		Credit
(h)	600—		

Office Supplies

	Debit		Credit
(c)	225—		
(f)	175—		
(BAL)	400—		

Office Equipment

	Debit		Credit
(b)	650—		

Truck

	Debit		Credit
(e)	12000—		

Accounts Payable

	Debit		Credit
(i)	650—	(b)	650—
		(f)	175—
	650—		825—
		(BAL)	175—

Notes Payable

	Debit		Credit
		(e)	8000—

Fees Earned

	Debit		Credit
		(g)	500—
		(j)	1000—
		(BAL)	1500—

Rent Expense

	Debit		Credit
(d)	300—		

Kathleen O'Brien, Capital

	Debit		Credit
		(a)	12000—

K. O'Brien, Interior Decorator
Trial Balance
December 31, 19—

Account	Debit	Credit
Cash	$ 6725—	
Accounts Receivable	1000—	
Prepaid Insurance	600—	
Office Supplies	400—	
Office Equipment	650—	
Truck	12000—	
Accounts Payable		$ 175—
Notes Payable		8000—
Fees Earned		1500—
Rent Expense	300—	
Kathleen O'Brien, Capital		12000—
	21675—	21675—

PROBLEMS

(Answers on page 109)

1. Analyze the following transactions and prepare a general entry for each.

Mary Reynolds, a recent veterinary-school graduate, began private practice by engaging in the following transactions:

June	1	Dr. Reynolds deposited $5000 in a bank account opened in the name of the business.
	4	Purchased medical supplies for $800 in cash.
	7	Purchased medical equipment for $1200, making a $500 down payment.
	12	Provided veterinary services and received $250.
	16	Purchased additional medical supplies on credit, $80.
	21	Provided veterinary services on credit, and billed clients for $400.
	23	Paid for the $80 of medical supplies purchased on June 16.
	28	Received $200 from clients billed on June 21.
	30	Paid a utility bill for $100.

2. Post the general journal entries of Problem 1 to the general ledger accounts.

3. Using the information created in Problem 2, prepare a trial balance for Dr. Reynolds.

5

ENTRIES FOR A MERCHANDISING CONCERN

OBJECTIVES

After completing this chapter, you should be able to:

- Explain the difference between a service concern and a merchandising concern.
- Describe the purpose of each account used by a merchandising concern.
- Record transactions using the merchandising accounts.
- Create an income statement for a merchandising firm.

Every company we have looked at up to this point has sold a service to its customers. Examples of service enterprises are law firms, barber shops, real estate brokers, dentists, and movie theaters. None of these companies sells a product. Merchandising concerns, on the other hand, specialize in buying physical goods from one company and selling them to customers at a profit. In fact, most of your personal business transactions are probably with merchandising concerns such as supermarkets, candy stores, or department stores.

The Service Co.
Income Statement
For the Year Ending December 31, 19__

	1	2
REVENUES		
Fees Earned		$15000—
OPERATING EXPENSES		
Rent Expense	$6000—	
Utilities Expense	3000—	
Office Supplies Expense	1000—	
Total Operating Expenses		10000—
Net Income		$5000—

In a service concern, it is fairly easy to calculate the firm's profit or loss from operations. The income statement would show the revenues earned over a specific period of time from which the operating expenses are subtracted. (See page 31 for a sample income statement of a service concern.)

Once we introduce a physical product into the picture, the calculation of a net profit or loss becomes a bit more complex. Look over the following income statement for a merchandising company. While it may look complicated, it is really very similar to the income statement of the service company.

The Trading Co.
Income Statement
For the Year Ending December 31, 19__

	1	2	3	4
REVENUES				
Gross Sales				$104000 —
LESS: Sales Returns and Allowances			$1000 —	
Sales Discounts			3000 —	4000 —
Net Sales				$100000 —
COST OF GOODS SOLD				
Beginning Merchandise Inventory Jan 1, 19__			$10000 —	
Purchases		$63000 —		
LESS: Purchase Returns and Allowances	$400 —			
Purchase Discounts	1600 —	2000 —		
Net Purchases			61000 —	
Merchandise Available for Sale			$71000 —	
Ending Merchandise Inventory Dec. 31, 19__			−11000 —	
Cost of Goods Sold				60000 —
Gross Profit on Sales				$40000 —
OPERATING EXPENSES				
Rent Expense			$10000 —	
Utilities Expense			3000 —	
Office Supplies Expense			2000 —	
Advertising Expense			3000 —	
Total Operating Expenses				20000 —
Net Income				$20000 —

If we analyze each section of the merchandising income statement, we can see why this format is necessary and we can introduce some new journal entries.

Revenues

Sales. This is the principal revenue account for a merchandising concern and, like any other revenue account, it is usually credited and has a normal credit balance.

1. *Cash Sale.* Sales recorded on a cash register are usually recorded at the end of the day with an entry similar to this:

Feb. 15	Cash	640—	
	Sales		640—

2. *Credit Sale.* An entry to record a credit sale would look like this:

Feb. 15	Accounts Receivable	640—	
	Sales		640—

Sales Returns and Allowances. This account is used to record the value of the goods returned by dissatisfied customers. It is normally debited because it is receiving the debit that "should have" been recorded in the Sales account. Logically, one could reason that if the Sales account is credited when the sale is made, then it should be debited when the merchandise is returned. If we did this, however, the amount of the returns would be lost in the Sales account. Therefore, we set up the Sales Returns and Allowances account to show management the value of the goods returned in relation to the amount of total sales. It serves as an "index of dissatisfaction" by telling management how dissatisfied their customers are with their products. On the income statement, it is subtracted from gross sales in arriving at the net sales amount. A sales return of $60 would be recorded like this:

Feb. 6	Sales Returns and Allowances	60—	
	Accounts Receivable (or Cash)		60—

Sales Returns and Allowances is known as a *contra* account. This type of account is used to preserve some balance which would be lost if it were recorded in some other account. The word "contra" is from Latin and means "against." The balance of a contra account is working against some other account. If the other account has a normal credit balance, its contra account will have a debit balance, and vice-versa. Another characteristic of the contra account is that it is inseparable from the primary account. Wherever you see the main account, you will usually see its contra account. On financial statements, the contra account is always subtracted from the main account. This is another example of the two accounts working "against" each other.

Sales Discounts. When goods are sold on credit, the seller sometimes offers the buyer a cash discount on the cost of the goods if payment is received by a certain date. If the terms 2/10, n/30 are written on the bill, the seller is telling the buyer he can deduct 2% from the cost of the merchandise if he pays within 10 days of the date of the bill. When the buyer does not pay within the discount period, he must pay the total amount within 30 days. If the buyer pays within the discount period, the seller must debit Sales Discounts for the amount deducted by the buyer. These discounts are accumulated in the Sales Discounts account until the end of the accounting period and then subtracted from gross sales to arrive at the net sales. This is because the discounts reduce the revenue received by the firm.

If the Canada Co. offers credit terms of 2/10, n/30 on an April 2, $1000 sale of tools to the Santa Monica Hardware Co., the Canada Co. entries would look like this:

SALE OF GOODS

Date	Account	Debit	Credit
Feb. 2	Accounts Receivable	1000–	
	Sales		1000–

PAYMENT WITHIN DISCOUNT PERIOD

Date	Account	Debit	Credit
Feb. 12	Cash	980–	
	Sales Discount	20–	
	Accounts Receivable		1000–

PAYMENT MADE ON LAST DAY OF CREDIT PERIOD

Date	Account	Debit	Credit
Mar. 4	Cash	1000–	
	Accounts Receivable		1000–

Cost of Goods Sold

The goods which were sold to produce revenue for the firm had to be purchased from a supplier. The purpose of this section is to determine the amount paid for this merchandise. When the cost of goods sold is subtracted from the net sales amount, the difference is the company's gross profit on sales. This is profit arising *only* from the buying and selling of merchandise.

Beginning Merchandise Inventory. This is the value of the merchandise in the warehouse at the beginning of the accounting period. It is available for resale to customers. Its value is based on what it cost to purchase the goods. Merchandise Inventory is an asset account and appears on the balance sheet.

Purchases. Merchandise bought during the accounting period is debited to the Purchases account. Remember, the term *merchandise* refers exclusively to goods that the company buys with the intention of reselling at a profit. Therefore, office supplies or store equipment would not be considered merchandise since they are not intended for resale. The Purchases account is debited only for the purchase of merchandise. If a company buys $20,000 of merchandise on account from the manufacturer, the entry would be recorded like this:

Date	Account	Debit	Credit
Feb. 14	Purchases	20000–	
	Accounts Payable		20000–

Purchase Returns and Allowances. This is very similar to the Sale Returns and Allowances contra account. It too is an "index of dissatisfaction," only this time it shows management how dissatisfied the company is with the merchandise being shipped by the suppliers. If the amount in this account is high relative to the purchases made, it may indicate that the suppliers are shipping inferior goods to the company. The normal balance for this account is a credit balance since it is receiving the credit that would have been used to reduce the amount in the Purchases account. If goods are returned to the supplier, we cannot consider it to be a purchase any longer. This is why the purchase returns and allowances is subtracted from purchases to arrive at net purchases. If $400 of the purchase in the last transaction is returned as being defective, the transaction is recorded as:

Feb. 20	Accounts Payable	400—	
	Purchase Returns and Allowances		400—

Purchase Discounts. This cash discount is the mirror image of the sales discount. What is a sales discount to the seller is a purchase discount to the buyer of merchandise. The buyer who takes advantage of an offered discount reduces his cost of purchases. This is why we see purchase discounts subtracted from purchases on the income statement and why the account has a normal credit balance, which is opposite that of Purchases. Earlier, we analyzed a transaction in which the Canada Co. offered credit terms of 2/10, n/30 on a $1000 sale to the Santa Monica Hardware Co. At that time we looked at the entries as they appeared on the Canada Co. Books. Now, we will see how the Santa Monica Hardware Co. records the transactions.

PURCHASE OF GOODS

Feb. 2	Purchases	1000—	
	Accounts Payable		1000—

PAYMENT WITHIN DISCOUNT PERIOD

Feb. 11	Accounts Payable	1000—	
	Purchase Discounts		20—
	Cash		980—

PAYMENT MADE ON LAST DAY OF CREDIT PERIOD

Mar. 4	Accounts Payable	1000—	
	Cash		1000—

Net Purchases. This is the final cost of all the purchases made during the accounting period. We started with the amount in the Purchases account, but then reduced this by the amount of the merchandise returned to the suppliers and the amount of discounts received from the early payment of bills.

Merchandise Available for Sale. This is the amount of merchandise we could have sold. At the beginning of the year, there was $10,000 worth of merchandise in the warehouse. During the year, the company bought an additional $61,000 of merchandise. Therefore, $71,000 of goods are available for sale if customers want to buy them.

Ending Merchandise Inventory. This is the value of the merchandise remaining in the warehouse at the end of the accounting period. It therefore represents the cost value of merchandise that could have been sold but was not. It will become the beginning merchandise inventory for the next accounting period.

Cost of Goods Sold. When the value of the merchandise left in the warehouse is subtracted from the goods that were available for sale, we find the cost of the goods that were sold. In other words, the company bought merchandise for $60,000 and sold it for $100,000.

Gross Profit on Sales. This is the profit generated from the buying and selling of merchandise.

Operating Expenses

These are the goods and services consumed by the company to produce the amount of net sales shown in the revenue section excluding the cost of merchandise sold. When these operating expenses are subtracted from the Gross Profit on Sales, we are left with a net profit or net loss for the accounting period.

PROBLEMS

(Answers on page 110)

1. Prepare general journal entries to record the following sales-related transactions:

April 8 Sold merchandise on credit to Peter Miller, terms 2/10, n/30, $2000.
10 Peter Miller returned $200 of defective merchandise.
13 Sold merchandise on credit to John Gordon, terms 2/10, n/30, $1000.
18 Peter Miller paid for the merchandise purchased on April 8, less the return and the discount (*Note:* The discount applies only to the merchandise kept by Mr. Miller.)
24 Sold merchandise for cash, $80.
30 John Gordon paid for the merchandise purchased on April 13.

2. Prepare general journal entries to record the following purchase-related transactions:

Aug. 1 Purchased merchandise on credit from the Panessa Corp., terms 2/10, n/30, $1100.
3 Returned for credit $100 of damaged merchandise received from the Panessa Corp.
7 Purchased merchandise for cash, $160.
9 Purchased merchandise on credit from the Coleman Co., terms 1/10, n/30, $1800.

11 Paid for the merchandise purchased from the Panessa Corp. on August 1, less the return and the discount.

31 Paid for the merchandise purchased from the Coleman Co. on August 9.

6

SUBSIDIARY LEDGERS AND SPECIAL JOURNALS

OBJECTIVES

After completing this chapter, you should be able to:

- Explain the advantages of using subsidiary ledgers.
- Discuss the relationship between controlling and subsidiary accounts.
- Create a schedule to prove the balance in a controlling account.
- Explain how special journals simplify the recording and posting of transactions.
- Identify the type of transaction recorded in each special journal.
- Record transactions in the special journals and post to the general ledger and subsidiary ledger accounts.

ADVANTAGES OF SUBSIDIARY LEDGERS

In the earlier chapters, we processed transactions by recording them in the general journal and then posting them to the general ledger accounts. At this point, we want to use two additional ledgers, called subsidiary ledgers, to simplify the posting process. In addition to the general ledger, we will now use an accounts receivable ledger and an accounts payable ledger. The advantages of using these ledgers are:

1. *Less detail in the general ledger.* Information which would ordinarily appear in a limited number of general ledger accounts can be transferred to many subsidiary accounts. This dispersion of detail information helps to keep the general ledger accounts uncluttered and makes it easier for the bookkeeper to maintain the accounts.
2. *Encourage division of labor.* The use of multiple ledgers allows one bookkeeper to work on the general ledger while others work on the subsidiary ledgers.

ACCOUNTS RECEIVABLE LEDGER

The first subsidiary ledger we will look at is the accounts receivable ledger. You recall from our earlier work that a $1000 sale of merchandise on credit would generate the following entry:

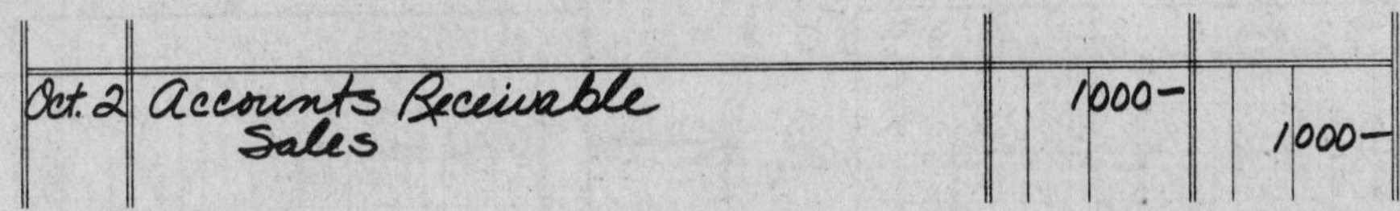

This entry, however, lacks an important piece of information. It does not identify the person or company that owed us the $1000. In order to correct the situation we must (a) name the customer in the journal entry and (b) create an individual account for each customer to keep accurate control over all money owed us. These individual accounts are kept in a separate book or card tray called a subsidiary ledger. The accounts in the subsidiary ledger are organized in alphabetical order, in contrast to general ledger accounts, which are arranged according to their order of appearance on the financial statements.

Returning to our original transaction, let us assume that we sold the $1000 of merchandise on credit to the Hart Corp.

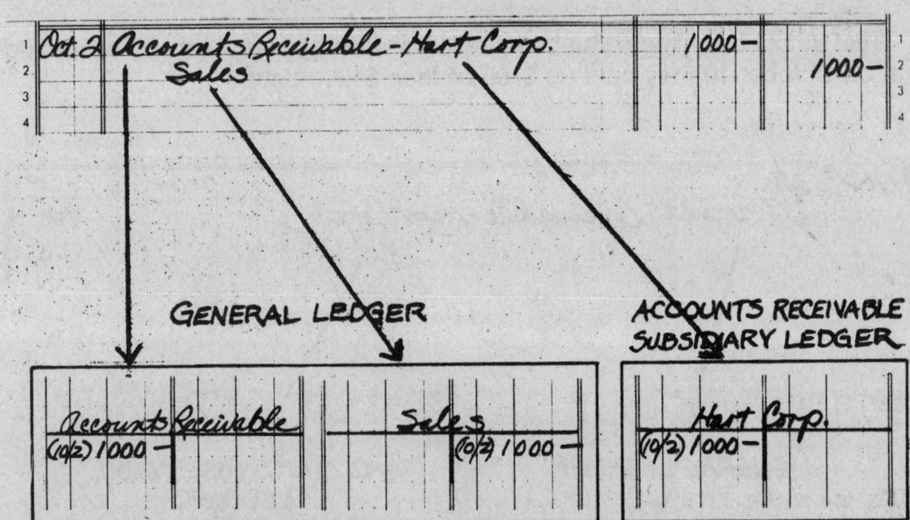

By establishing an individual account for the Hart Corp., we have separated them from all other customers. This detail information is no longer buried in the Accounts Receivable account, and we can now more easily determine how much they owe us.

You may be wondering if this procedure violates the principle that there must be equal debits and credits in every transaction. It sure does look that way, since we made two debits, totaling $2000, but only one credit for $1000. Despite its appearance, we have maintained equality. The Accounts Receivable account in the general ledger is our primary or *controlling* account, while the individual customer account is a secondary or *subsidiary* account which merely *describes* the entry recorded in the controlling account. If all postings have been correctly recorded, the balance in the controlling account should equal the total of the individual account balances in the subsidiary ledger.

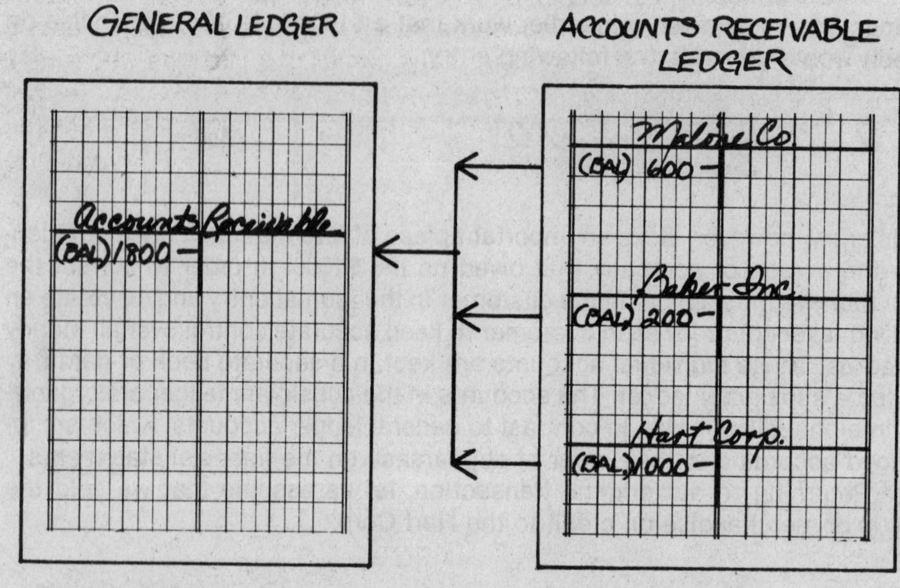

Let us continue the sequence of events with the Hart Corp. by assuming that on October 10 they paid us $700 of their $1000 debt.

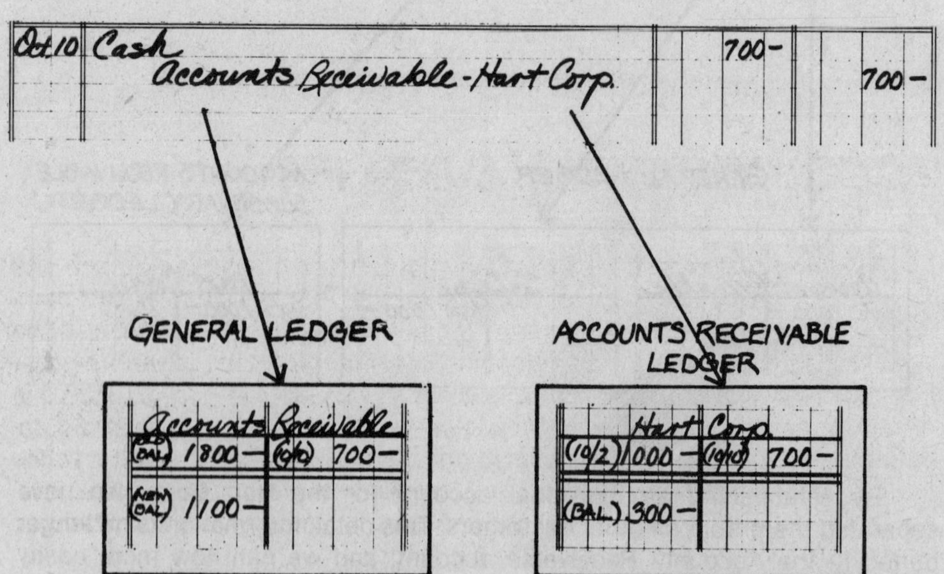

The controlling account now shows that we are entitled to receive $1100 from our customers. The Hart Corp. subsidiary account shows that they owe $300 of the $1100 receivable from our customers. If we wish to prove this amount, we can create a formal statement which will show us exactly who owes us this money.

SCHEDULE OF ACCOUNTS RECEIVABLE

The balances in the accounts receivable ledger may be summarized in a report known as a Schedule of Accounts Receivable. This statement is easy to construct because it is only a listing of the names of customers who owe us money and the amount each owes. It is important, however, that the total from the schedule agrees with the balance in the Accounts Receivable account.

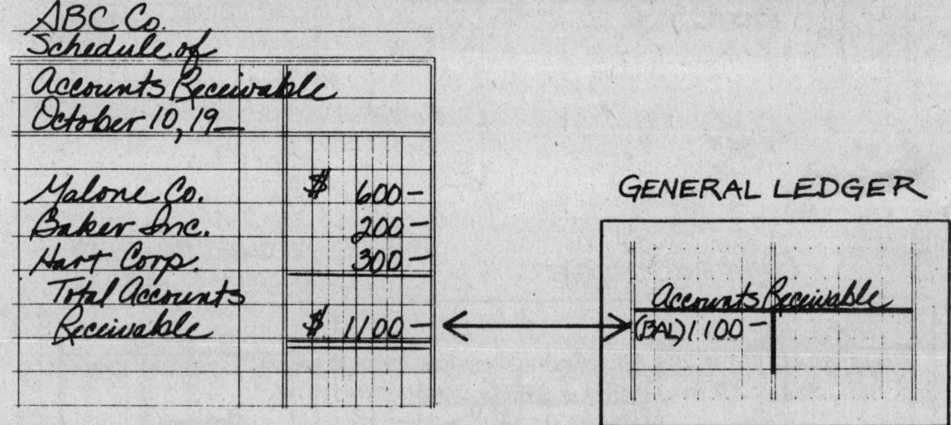

ACCOUNTS PAYABLE LEDGER

We have just seen how a company keeps track of who owes them and how much only by using an accounts receivable ledger. Naturally, this company also makes purchases on credit, thereby creating liabilities that must be paid. It is as important to maintain control over our accounts payable as over our accounts receivable. As you have probably guessed, the way to do this is to set up an accounts payable subsidiary ledger containing a separate account for each creditor. We must also specify the name of the creditor in the journal entry. If you trace the following transactions through the general journal to the ledgers, you will notice the very strong similarity to the procedures used to control the accounts receivable ledger.

<u>Transactions</u>

May	7	Purchased $600 of merchandise on credit from the B.D. Corp.
	9	Bought $1100 of furniture on credit from the Folsum Co.
	10	Purchased a word processing machine from Video Hut on credit for $4800.
	16	Paid $2000 of the $4800 owed to Video Hut.

		General Journal Entries	1	2
May	7	Purchases	600—	
		Accounts Payable-B.D. Corp.		600—
	9	Furniture	1100—	
		Accounts Payable-Tolsum Co.		1100—
	10	Office Equipment	4800—	
		Accounts Payable-Video Hut		4800—
	14	Accounts Payable-Video Hut	2000—	
		Cash		2000—

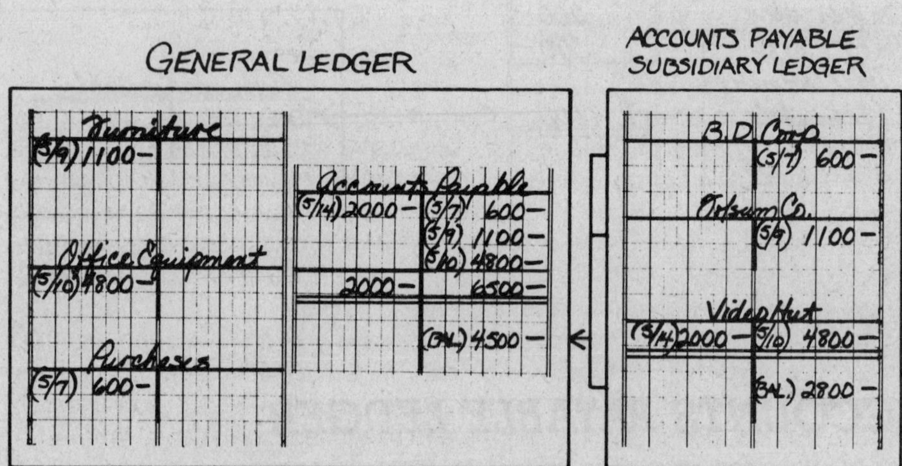

Observe that the individual subsidiary accounts identify the amount of money we owe to each of our creditors. Also notice that the final balance ($4500) in the controlling Accounts Payable account is equal to the sum of the individual account balances in the accounts payable subsidiary ledger.

Schedule of Accounts Payable

This statement is very similar to the Schedule of Accounts Receivable we prepared earlier. In this case, it is a listing of the individual creditors and the amount of money we owe them. As before, the total of the individual accounts must equal the balance in the controlling account.

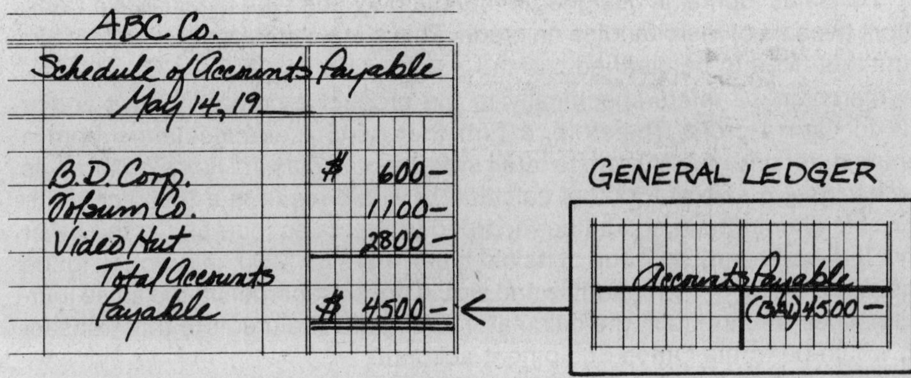

THE NEED FOR SPECIAL JOURNALS

The first part of this chapter attempted to simplify the accounting process through the use of the accounts receivable and accounts payable subsidiary ledgers. We continue this process by turning our attention to the way transactions are recorded in the general journal. It is not particularly difficult to write a few general journal entries, but this recording procedure turns out to be very slow and cumbersome when hundreds or thousands of similar transactions are recorded over a month's time.

It is possible to reduce the writing and posting effort by grouping similar transactions together and recording them in a special journal specifically designed to handle them with a minimum of effort. We will now classify repetitive transactions into four groups and use a separate special journal for each type of transaction. The general journal will continue to be used when a transaction cannot be recorded in one of the special journals.

JOURNAL	TYPE OF TRANSACTION	POSTING SYMBOL
Sales Journal	Sales of merchandise on credit	S
Purchases Journal	Purchases of merchandise on credit	P
Cash Receipts Journal	Receipts of cash	CR
Cash Payments Journal	Payments of cash	CP
General Journal	All transactions which cannot be categorized into one of the above classes	J

The advantages of using special journals include a reduction in the labor needed to write each transaction, fewer postings to the general ledger accounts, and a better division of labor because each special journal can be handled by a different bookkeeper.

SALES JOURNAL

The sales journal is designed to handle only one type of repetitive transaction: the sale of merchandise on credit. This simple statement contains two terms that need to be clarified.

Merchandise refers specifically to the product a company buys and/or sells to earn a profit. Therefore, a firm that purchases calculators from a manufacturer and resells them to retail stores would classify its calculators as merchandise. A sale of $5000 of calculators would result in a $5000 credit to the Sales account and should be recorded in the sales journal. On the other hand, if the company sold one of its old typewriters for $200, this would not be considered a sale of merchandise and would not be recorded in the sales journal because the firm is in the calculator business. The credit in this transaction would be to the Office Equipment account.

Only credit sales of merchandise should be recorded in the sales journal. A sale of merchandise for cash would be recorded in the cash receipts journal, not the sales journal.

Whenever a transaction involving the credit sale of merchandise is recorded in the general journal, the entry has the following format:

Accounts Receivable (Customer's name)	XXX	
Sales		XXX

If a firm had 25 credit sales in one day, this entry would be repeated 25 times. If we look closely at these transactions, we find that a substantial portion of each entry is repetitive in nature. Every entry has a debit to Accounts Receivable and a credit to Sales. Only the customer's name and the amount will vary from transaction to transaction. The sales journal takes advantage of this fact by recording and posting the variable information on a day-to-day basis. The fixed data (Accounts Receivable—debit/Sales—credit) is posted only once, at the end of the month.

In the illustration on page 45, we use four credit sales transactions to represent all such transactions for the month of February.

The specific procedures for recording and posting the sales journal are:

1. In the sales journal, record the date, customer name, invoice number and amount.
2. Post the amount as a debit to the customer's account in the accounts receivable ledger. Then place a check-mark in the Posting Reference column of the sales journal. A cross-reference is created when the letter **S** (sales journal) followed by the page number is entered in the Posting Reference column of the subsidiary account.
3. At the end of the month, total the Amount column and post as a debit to Accounts Receivable and a credit to Sales. Below the sales journal total, record the numbers of the general ledger accounts receiving the postings. Record the journal symbol and page number in the Posting Reference column of the general ledger accounts.

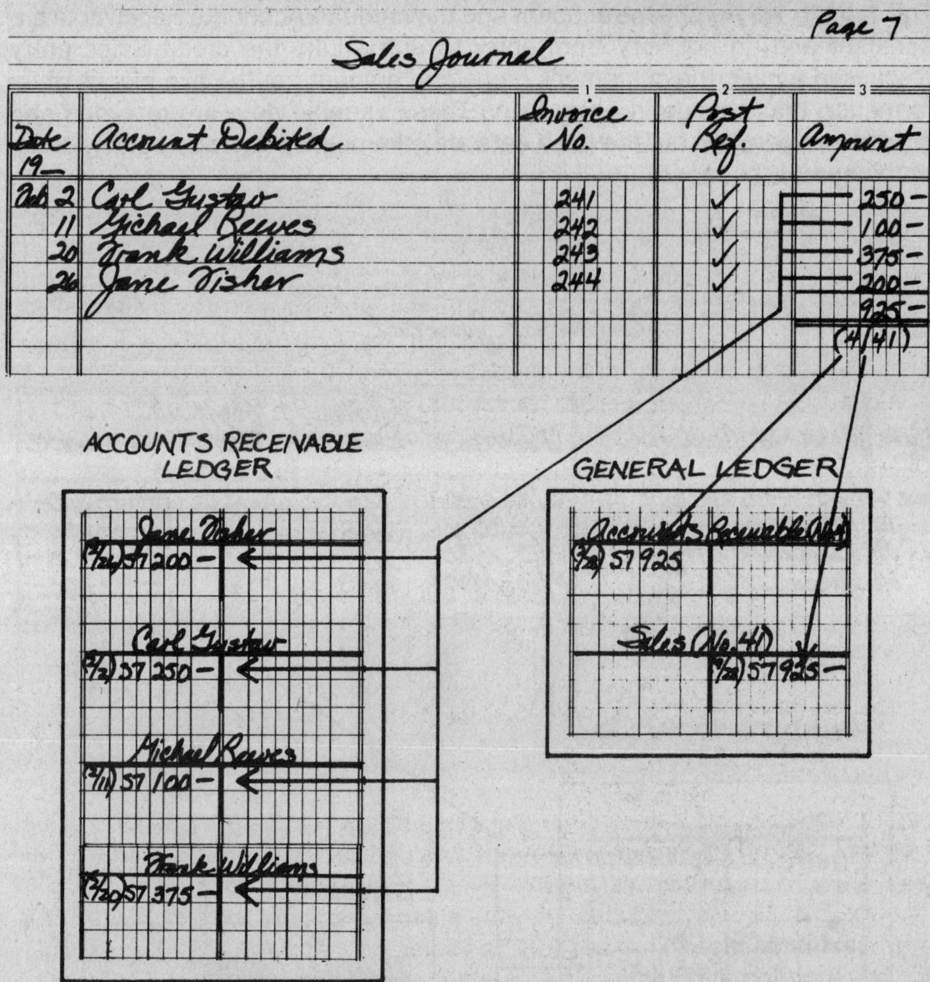

PURCHASES JOURNAL

This journal handles only purchases of merchandise on credit. A cash purchase of merchandise would be recorded in the cash payments journal. We will see that the procedures associated with the purchases journal are very similar to those of the sales journal.

Every transaction involving a credit purchase of merchandise has the same basic entry when recorded in the general journal.

Purchases	XXX	
Accounts Payable (Creditor's name)		XXX

The debit to the Purchases account and the credit to Accounts Receivable are constant and do not vary from entry to entry. Like the credit Sales entry discussed earlier, the customer's name and amount are the two pieces of information that change in each entry. These variable data are recorded and posted immediately, but the fixed data are summarized and posted only once, at the end of the month.

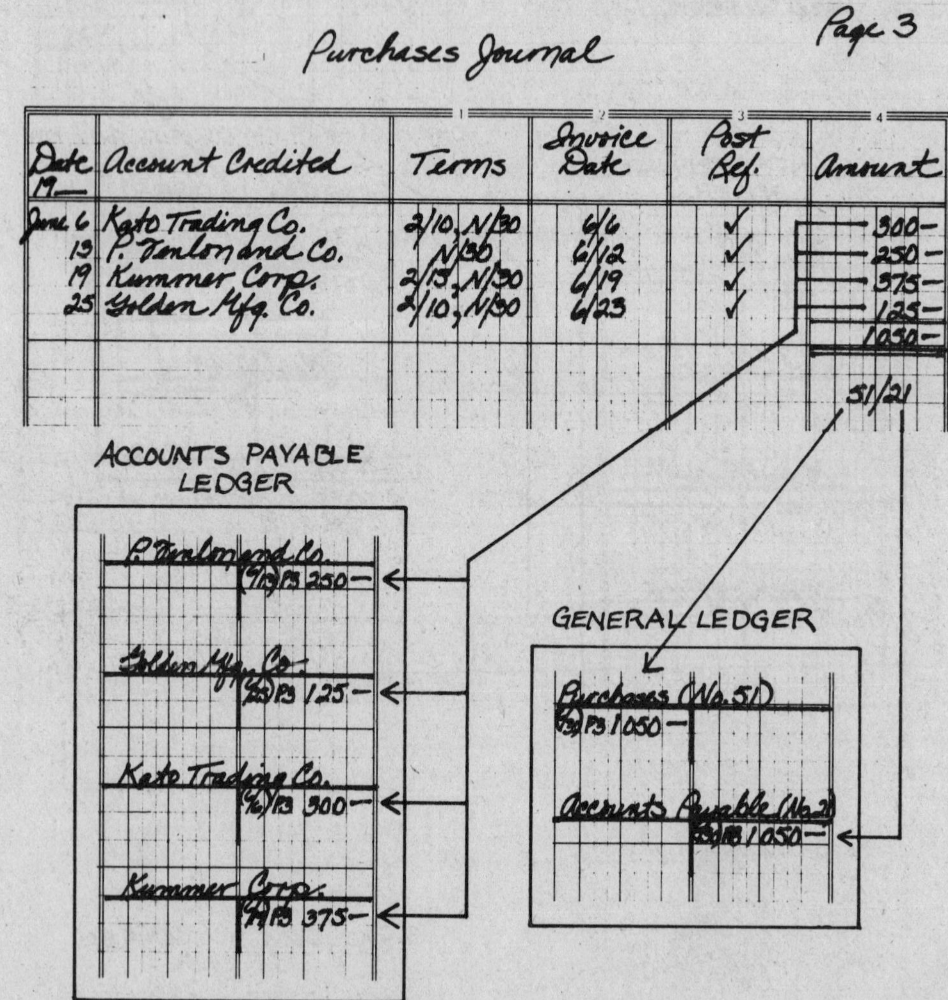

The detail steps for recording and posting the purchases journal are:

1. Record the date, creditor's name, cash discount terms, date and amount of the invoice in the purchases journal.
2. Post the amount as a credit to the creditor's account in the accounts payable ledger and enter the posting references.
3. On the last day of the month, add and post the total amount as a debit to Purchases and a credit to Accounts Payable.

CASH RECEIPTS JOURNAL

This journal is designed to handle *all* receipts of cash. The cash receipts journal is different from the other special journals we have looked at because it has several columns, not just one. A multicolumn journal is necessary because, although the debit is always to the Cash account, the credit may be to a variety of accounts. The general journal format will illustrate the fixed and variable portions of the typical cash receipts entry.

Cash	XXX	
(One or more credits)		XXX

Since cash is involved in each transaction, one of the columns must be used to record this debit. Also, because frequent sources of cash include cash sales and receipts from customers who pay their accounts, a credit column is established for each of these frequently occurring events. It would not be effi-

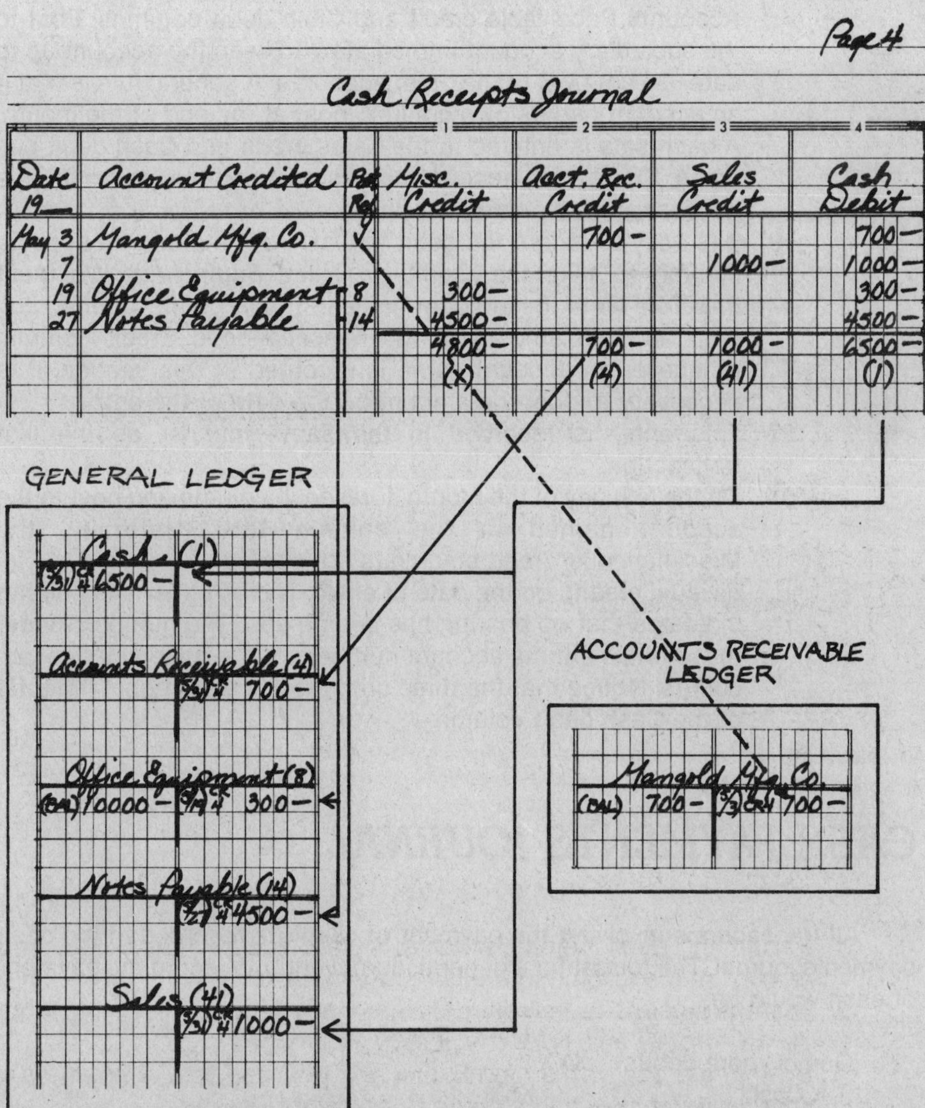

cient to set up a column for every credit that could occur. Thus, only one Miscellaneous Credit column is used for all other credits.

Trace each of the following transactions through the cash receipts journal to the ledger accounts (see illustration on page 47).

Transactions

May 3 Received $700 from the Mangold Mfg. Co. in full payment of a previous sale.
7 Sold $1000 of merchandise for cash.
19 Sold a typewriter for $300 cash.
27 Borrowed $4500 from the First State Bank by giving a promissory note.

The recording and posting of the cash receipts journal can be summarized by transaction date as follows:

May 3 When cash is received from a customer, record the company name in the Account Credited column and the amount in the Accounts Receivable credit and Cash debit columns. Post to the subsidiary account immediately to keep the account up to date. Do not post to the other accounts. A general rule is that if an account has its own column, post at the end of the month.
7 A cash sale is entered in the Sales credit and Cash debit columns. Since each account has its own column, no posting is necessary at this time.
19 It is easy to record the debit to Cash, but there is no specific column to take the credit to Office Equipment. We must therefore write the account name in the Account Credited column and the amount in the Miscellaneous Credit column. Whenever an account name is recorded in this section, it is necessary to post the amount on the date of the entry.
27 This entry is recorded in the same manner as the last transaction.
31 On the last day of the month, total each column and post to the account named in the column title. Naturally, the Miscellaneous Credit column is not posted. We posted the individual credits on the date of entry. The (x) under this column indicates that no posting has been made. The numbers under these totals are the account numbers of the general ledger accounts. Notice that the three credit totals must equal the total of the Cash debit column.

CASH PAYMENTS JOURNAL

All transactions involving the payment of cash are recorded in the cash payments journal. The format for a general journal entry to record the payment of cash would be:

(One or more debits)	XXX	
Cash		XXX

The Cash account is always credited, but there may be a debit to one or more accounts. Therefore, a cash payments journal should have a Cash credit column and debit columns for those entries that occur most often.

Once again you should trace the following transactions through the cash payments journal to the ledger accounts. You will see that the techniques of recording are very similar to those employed in the cash receipts journal.

Transactions

July	6	Paid the Kato Trading Co. $300 for the June 6 purchase. (This was previously recorded in the purchases journal.)
	14	Paid for a newspaper advertisement in the *Daily Post*, $125.
	23	Purchased merchandise for cash, $220.
	30	Paid the monthly salary of two employees, $2800.

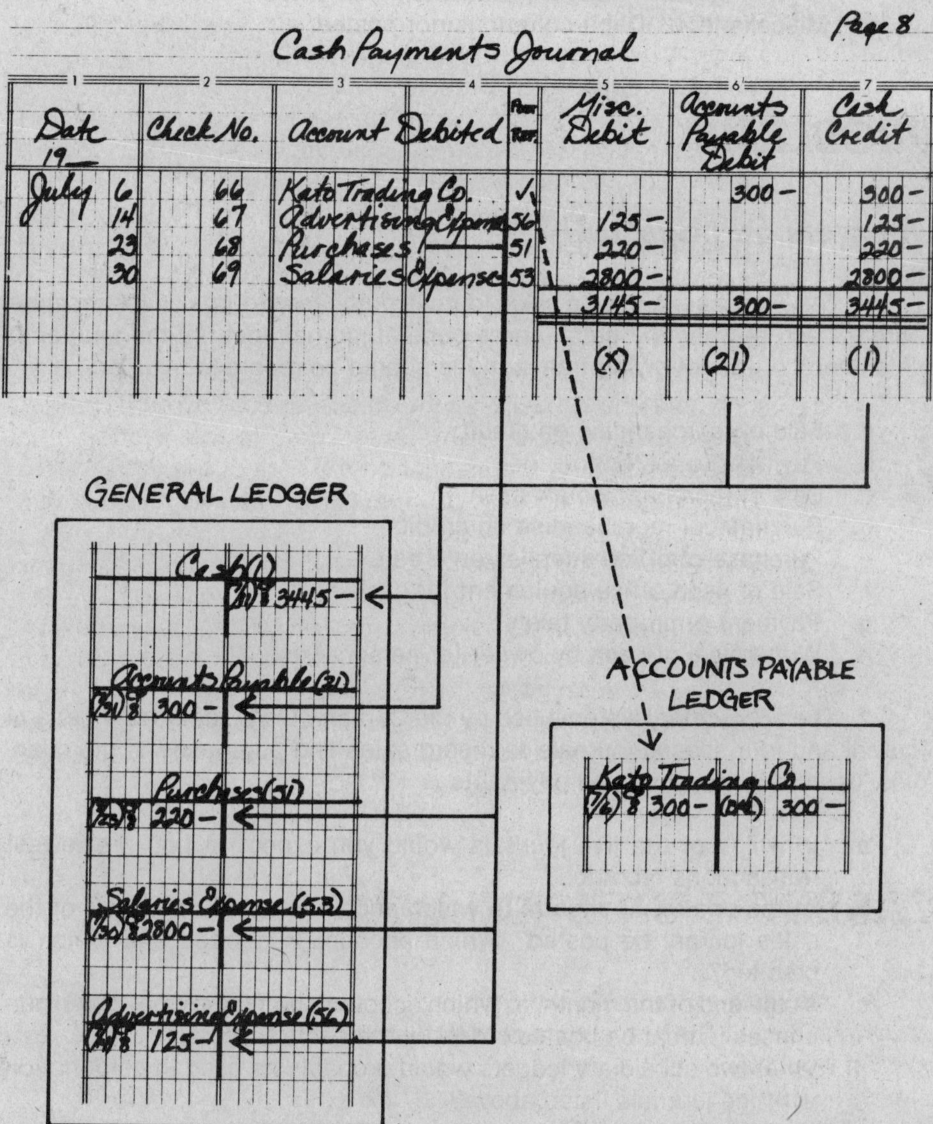

The procedure for recording the cash payments journal closely resembles that used with the cash receipts journal:

1. A check is written every time a cash payment is made, and the check number recorded in the cash payments journal. This serves as a convenient reference and control over cash.
2. If a cash payment is made to reduce an existing liability, the name of the creditor is recorded in the Account Debited section and posted immediately to the subsidiary account. The amount is recorded in the Accounts Payable debit column and, naturally, in the Cash credit column.
3. If the debit cannot be recorded in a column reserved for a specific account, it is written in the Account Debited and Miscellaneous Debit sections and posted daily.
4. At the end of the month, the columns are added and the total posted to the general ledger accounts. Remember, the total of the Miscellaneous Debit column is not posted.

PROBLEMS

(Answers on page 111)

1. The Ramsey Co. uses a sales journal, purchases journal, cash receipts journal, cash payments journal, and a general journal. Identify the journal in which each of the following transactions should be recorded.

- **a.** Sale of merchandise on credit.
- **b.** Payment to a creditor.
- **c.** Sale of merchandise for cash.
- **d.** Purchase of merchandise on credit.
- **e.** Purchase of office supplies on credit.
- **f.** Sale of used office equipment for cash.
- **g.** Payment of property taxes.
- **h.** Withdrawal of cash by owner for personal use.

2. The accounting system used by the Carberry Corp. includes a general journal and four special journals to record sales and purchases of merchandise, cash receipts, and cash payments.

- **a.** In which of the five journals would you expect to find the fewest transactions recorded?
- **b.** At the end of the month, to which accounts should the total of the sales journal be posted? Which account is debited and which is credited?
- **c.** At the end of the month, to which account should the total of the purchases journal be posted? Identify the debit and credit.
- **d.** What two subsidiary ledgers would probably be used in conjunction with the journals listed above?

7

CONTROLLING CASH

OBJECTIVES

After completing this chapter, you should be able to:

- Define *cash* from an accounting point of view.
- Describe the types of documents used to maintain a checking account.
- Write blank, full, and restrictive check endorsements and explain the advantages or disadvantages of each.
- Explain why a bank reconciliation is needed.
- Prepare a bank reconciliation statement.
- Explain the steps involved in establishing and maintaining a petty cash fund.
- Record the journal entries necessary to create and maintain a petty cash fund.

CASH

In many firms, the Cash account is debited or credited more frequently than any other account. You may be thinking of cash as being only bills and coins. From an accounting point of view, however, we must say that cash is any medium of exchange which will be accepted by a bank for deposit and will be added to the depositor's account. Some examples of cash are:

coins	personal checks
paper money	bank drafts
savings account balances	cashier's checks
checking account balances	money orders

Cash, by its very nature, is more vulnerable to theft than any other asset. It is therefore extremely important that cash be safeguarded by effective internal controls. One fundamental principle of internal control is that all payments be made by check.

USING THE CHECKING ACCOUNT TO CONTROL CASH

Banking institutions provide a number of important services to the business community. In addition to safeguarding the firm's cash, they also provide checking accounts which are used to control cash receipts and cash disbursements. A major advantage of paying all bills by check is that a double set of records is maintained. The business firm has a checkbook record, along with other supporting documents, showing when and to whom the cash was paid. Once each month the bank provides a written statement to the firm which shows all checks paid and all deposits received by the bank since the last statement. Furthermore, the cancelled checks are returned by the bank, which provides legal proof that payment has been made.

CHECKING ACCOUNT FORMS

There are several forms used in maintaining a checking account. Among these are:

1. *Signature Card:* This card is signed by the depositor when the checking account is opened and it is kept by the bank to verify signatures on subsequently drawn checks.
2. *Deposit Slip:* Each time a deposit is made, a deposit slip (Figure 7-1) is created in duplicate and presented to the bank teller along with the items to be deposited. The teller will stamp and return one of the deposit slips, which then serves as written evidence of the date and amount of the deposit.

DEPOSITED TO THE CREDIT OF

ACCOUNT NUMBER

ACCOUNT NAME

DATE ____________

	DOLLARS	CENTS
BILLS		
COIN COUPONS		
CHECKS		
TOTAL FROM OTHER SIDE		
TOTAL		

Figure 7-1. Bank Deposit Slip

3. *Check:* A check (Figure 7-2) is a written order, signed by the depositor, directing the bank to pay a specified amount of money to the person named on the check. There are three parties involved in every check:
   Drawer: the person who writes the check.
   Drawee: the bank on which the check is drawn.
   Payee: the one to whom the check is to be paid.

981

______________ 19 ____

PAY TO THE ORDER OF ______________________________ $ ________

____ DOLLARS

MEMO ______________________________ ______________________________

Figure 7-2. Check

4. *Bank Statement:* The bank statement (Figure 7-3) is the bank's record of all activity in the checking account during the past month. All statements show the customer's beginning balance, additions to

HOUSTON **National**

Pisani Corp.
500 Irvington Road
Houston, Texas 77027

Account Number 12345678
Statement Closing Date 10-15-XX
Page 1 ENCLOSURES 17
CHECKS 17 DEPOSITS 5

CHECKING STATEMENT

PREVIOUS BALANCE	+ TOTAL CREDITS	- TOTAL DEBITS	- SERVICE CHRG	= NEW BALANCE
2,509.69	3,731.00	1,802.73	.00	4,437.96

CHECKS AND OTHER DEBITS			CREDITS	DATE	BALANCE
OPENING BALANCE				09-15	2,509.69
144.00				09-15	2,365.69
100.00					
			635.00		
			590.00		
			1,515.00		
			10.000M	09-28	5,015.69
47.35	68.02	74.92		09-30	4,825.40
47.00	52.88	75.08			
106.37				10-01	4,544.07
38.77	87.68	262.26		10-02	4,155.36
534.17				10-05	3,621.19
56.70			981.00	10-06	4,545.49
3.03				10-08	4,542.46
89.50				10-09	4,452.96
15.00				10-14	4,437.96

AD Loan Advance	EC Error Correction	MT Mortgage Payment	RI Returned Item	Savings Codes
BV Back Valued	FT Funds Transfer	OC Overdraft Charge	SC Service Charge	DP Deposit
CB Checkbook Charge	IN Interest	OD Overdraft	SS Social Security	ID Interest Disbursement
CC Certified Check	LS List Posted	PT Personal Trust Transfer	ST Savings Transfer	IN Interest
CM Credit Memo	LT Inst. Loan Payment	PY Payment To Loan	VT Visa Transaction	WD Withdrawal
DM Debit Memo				

Figure 7-3. Bank Statement

the account (credits), deductions from the account (debits), and the ending balance as of the closing date. Deposits are recorded as credits to the account since they increase the banks liability to the depositor. Similarly, when checks are paid by the bank, they are recorded as debits because they reduce the banks liability. *Credit memos* and *debit memos* are notifications by the bank that they have increased (credit) or decreased (debit) the account balance. A written explanation of the action taken is also supplied. On the statement date, the bank statement is prepared and mailed to the depositor along with the cancelled checks.

ENDORSING CHECKS

Whenever a check is deposited in an account, it must be endorsed or signed on the back by the depositor. In effect, this constitutes a transfer of ownership and provides certain legal guarantees of payment to the bank.

Endorsements may be hand-written or rubber-stamped and vary in their degree of completeness.

1. *Blank Endorsement* (Figure 7-4). This endorsement contains only the name of the depositor and involves the greatest risk if the check is lost or stolen. In effect, it makes the check payable to the bearer of the instrument even if that person merely found a lost check.

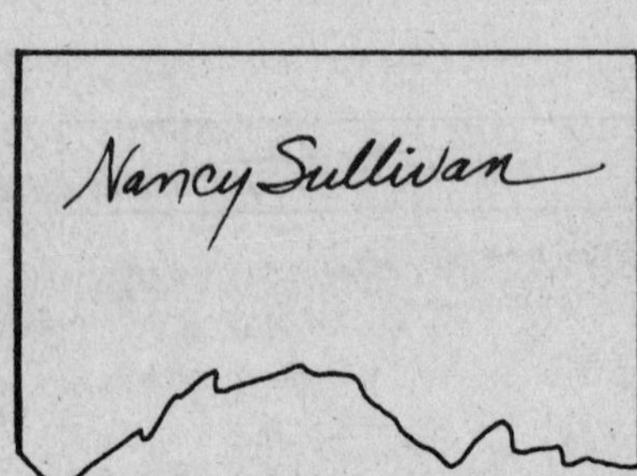

Figure 7-4. Bank Endorsement

2. *Endorsement in Full* (Figure 7-5). An endorsement in full specifies that the check is being transferred to the particular person or bank named in the endorsement.

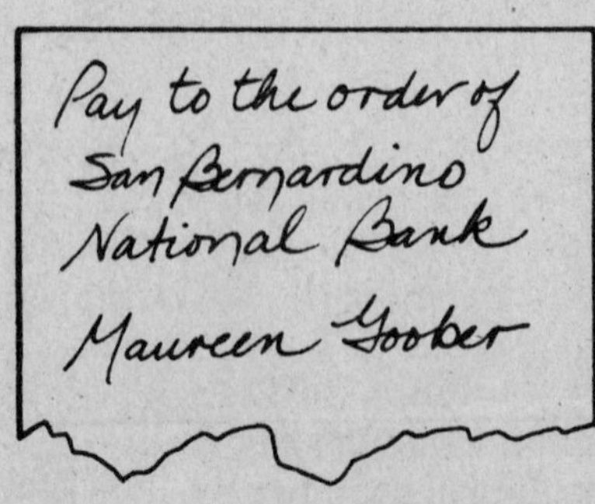

Figure 7-5. Endorsement in Full

3. *Restrictive Endorsement* (Figure 7-6). This type of endorsement is usually made when checks are prepared for deposit. Its principal advantage is that it limits what can be done with the check.

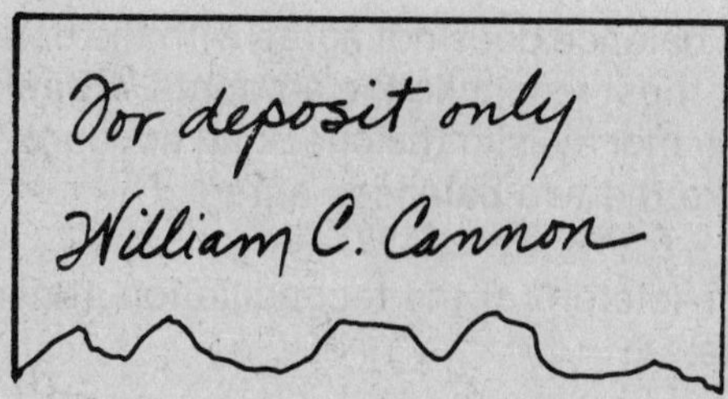

Figure 7-6. Restrictive Endorsement

WHY A BANK RECONCILIATION IS NEEDED

When the depositor receives a bank statement and compares the bank's cash balance with his own, they will probably not agree. This is not unusual. Some of the possible reasons for this disagreement are:

1. As of the statement closing date, the bank had no knowledge of a transaction entered into by the depositor. Examples are:
   Outstanding checks: The depositor has written checks and reduced the balance of his Cash account, but the checks have not yet been presented to the bank for payment.
   Deposit in transit: This occurs when the depositor has either mailed a deposit to the bank or made a deposit after closing hours in the bank's night depository. If the deposit arrives after the closing of business on the statement date, it will not appear on the statement.
2. The depositor had no knowledge of some action taken by the bank. He learned of the action from the entries recorded on the bank statement. Examples are:
   Service charges: These are amounts deducted for services provided by the bank. The depositor, however, usually does not know the exact amount until the bank statement arrives. At that time, the amount should be subtracted from the firm's cash balance.
   Collections: Banks will collect promissory notes for a fee and add the proceeds to the checking account. The depositor may not know of the collection until the bank statement arrives. Consequently, the amount of the proceeds must be added to the depositor's cash balance in order to agree with the bank balance.
3. An error has been made by either the depositor or the bank.

STEPS IN RECONCILING THE BANK BALANCE

If the firm's cash balance does not agree with the balance reported by the bank, the bookkeeper must reconcile the amounts. A bank reconciliation tells you exactly how much money is in the checking account. The following steps are necessary to make the two balances agree:

1. Create the "skeleton" of the reconciliation statement, which should look like this:

   NAME OF COMPANY
   BANK RECONCILIATION
   DATE

Book balance $	Bank balance $
ADD:	ADD:
DEDUCT:	DEDUCT:

   The "Book balance" is the amount of cash as recorded in the checkbook, and the "Bank balance" is the ending balance shown on the bank statement. These amounts are recorded next to the dollar signs. Although the shape of the reconciliation form bears a resemblance to the T account, it is not an account and is not debited or credited.
2. Compare the deposits recorded in the checkbook with those on the bank statement. If a deposit does not appear on the bank statement, record this amount on the "Bank balance" side in the "ADD" section.
3. Arrange the checks returned by the bank in numerical order and check off these items against the entries in the checkbook. Any check that has not been returned is an outstanding check and should be recorded on the "Bank balance" side in the "DEDUCT" section.
4. Compare the bank statement with the checkbook to see if the bank has levied a service charge that has not been recorded in the checkbook. If this has happened, deduct the amount from the "Book balance" amount. Use this procedure for any unrecorded deduction made by the bank.
5. If a promissory note has been collected by the bank but has not been recorded in the checkbook, add this amount on the "Book balance" side.
6. If an error has been made either by you or the bank, the error should be recorded on the side of the one who made the mistake. Since you want to correct the error, the amount should be entered in the section which will counteract the original error. For example, if the bank charged you a $10 fee for a service never performed, you would enter this in the "ADD" section of the bank balance side. It is added to counteract the original subtraction error.

7. When the checkbook and bank balances are equal, it is necessary to adjust the checkbook balance for *all* entries on the "Book balance" side. Otherwise, the checkbook will not contain the correct balance just calculated. It is also necessary to journalize and post all transactions which affect ledger accounts. If the bank charged a $7.50 service fee, the following entry would be recorded.

Miscellaneous Expense	$7.50	
Cash		$7.50

On the "Bank balance" side, you do not have to do anything unless the bank has made an error, in which case they must be notified so that it can be corrected.

If you are not sure on which side of the bank reconciliation to enter an amount, you can ask yourself, "Who knows about the item and who does not know about it?" The entry should be recorded on the side of the one who *does not know* the transaction has taken place. For example, the person who writes a check obviously knows of the existence of the check, but the bank has no knowledge of it until it is presented for payment. Therefore, the outstanding check must be recorded on the "Bank balance" side. This type of analysis will work for all transactions except those involving errors, but then we know that an error is always recorded on the side of the one who made the error.

The following problem will help to clarify what has been discussed so far.

On June 30, the bookkeeper for the Huron Corp. is attempting to reconcile the company's checkbook balance of $2420 with the bank statement balance of $2343. An analysis of both documents reveals the following:

1. A $500 deposit was made after banking hours on the closing date and consequently did not appear on the bank statement.
2. Two checks were not returned by the bank, No. 373 for $85 and No. 386 for $53.
3. The bank collected a $300 promissory note for Huron Corp. and deposited the amount in the checking account.
4. The bank charged $15 for services rendered.

Huron Corp.
Bank Reconciliation
June 30, 19__

Book balance	$2420 —	Bank balance	$2343 —
ADD:		ADD:	
Proceeds of note	300 —	Deposit in transit	500 —
	$2720 —		$2843 —
DEDUCT:		DEDUCT:	
Service charge	15 —	Outstanding checks:	
		No. 373 $85	
		No. 386 53	138 —
Corrected balance	$2705 —	Corrected balance	$2705 —

Once the correct cash balance has been determined, the proceeds of the note should be added and the service charge subtracted in the checkbook. The new checkbook balance should now be $2705.

Since these "Book balance" transactions affected ledger accounts, the following entries should also be noted:

Date		Account	1	2
June	30	Cash	300 —	
		Notes Receivable		300 —
	30	Miscellaneous Expense	15 —	
		Cash		15 —

THE PETTY CASH FUND

It was mentioned earlier that a basic principle of internal control is the payment of all bills by check. Situations arise, however, that require the immediate payment of small amounts of cash such as postage due, small purchases of office supplies, and the payment of collect telegrams. In order to monitor these transactions, a petty cash fund is established and a petty cashier appointed to make payments from the fund.

The steps involved in establishing and maintaining the fund are as follows:

1. *Establishing the fund.* When the fund is started, a check is drawn, cashed, and the proceeds kept by the petty cashier in a locked drawer. At the same time, a journal entry is made to record the establishment of the fund.

Date		Account		
June	15	Petty Cash	200 —	
		Cash		200 —

   This entry shows that the fund has been established and that its maximum balance is $200. We will see that this is one of the few times a debit or credit is made to the Petty Cash account. If the maximum balance were increased to $250 at a later date, we would debit the account for an additional $50, or if the balance were decreased to $150, the account would receive a $50 credit.

2. *Making payments from the fund.* Whenever a request for funds is made by an employee, a petty cash receipt (Figure 7-7) is signed by the person receiving the payment. In addition to the employee's signature, the receipt shows the date of payment, the amount and purpose of the disbursement, and the account to be debited. The amount recorded on the petty cash receipt is usually debited to some asset or expense account. Each time a cash payment is made, a petty cash receipt is placed in the cash drawer. It therefore follows

that the total of cash and receipts in the drawer should always equal the maximum balance.

PETTY CASH RECEIPT

No. ______________

Date ______________

Paid to ______________________________

For ______________________________

Charge to ______________________________

Amount ______________________________

______________________ Received by   ______________________ Approved by

Figure 7-7. Petty Cash Receipt

3. *Replenishing the fund.* Eventually, the fund will decline to a low level and must be brought up to the maximum balance. If our $200 fund declined to $25, the petty cashier would have $175 of receipts. These receipts would be given to the accounting department and a $175 check issued to bring the fund up to the maximum $200 level. (Remember that $25 is in the cash drawer.) Although the fund has been replenished, the payments have not been recorded in the ledger accounts. If we neglect to do this, the Cash account would be overstated, and various expense or asset accounts understated, by $175. We know that since $175 was paid, the cash balance must decrease by this amount. If we credit Cash for $175, we must have an equal amount of debits. These can be found by analyzing the petty cash receipts, which show the purpose of the payments and the accounts to be charged. Once the debits are known, the journal entry can be made.

Date	Account	Debit	Credit
July 10	Office Supplies	62—	
	Postage Expense	44—	
	Delivery Expense	50—	
	Miscellaneous Expense	19—	
	Cash		175—

Notice that the Petty Cash account was *not* debited. The balance in the Petty Cash account is still the original $200. We would debit or credit this account now only if we wanted to increase or decrease the original balance. For example, if we want to increase the maximum balance to $250, a second check would be drawn for $50 and the following entry made.

Date	Account	Debit	Credit
July 10	Petty Cash	50—	
	Cash		50—

Altogether, the petty cashier now has checks totaling $225, which, when added to the $25 remaining in the cash drawer, bring the fund up to the new maximum balance of $250.

PROBLEMS

(Answers on page 111)

1. **A.** Paul Saenger wishes to transfer a check to Steve Goldstein. Show how a full endorsement would be written.

   B. If Mr. Saenger wrote a blank endorsement, how would it be written?

   C. How would Mr. Saenger write a restrictive endorsement to deposit the check in the First State Bank?

A B C

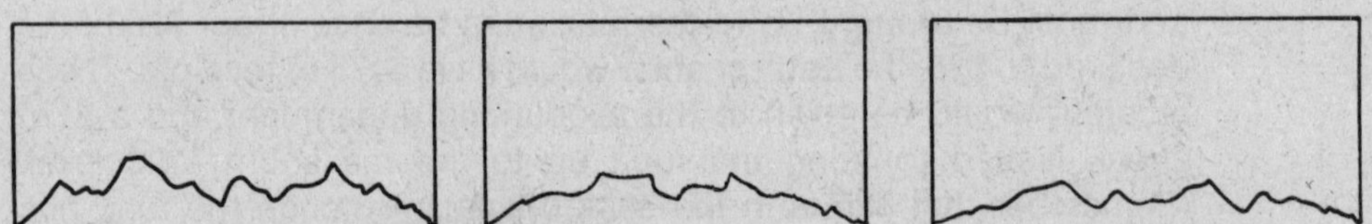

2. **A.** Use the following data to reconcile the bank account of the Connamara Marble Co. on December 31.
   - Check balance $2048.
   - Bank statement balance $3520.
   - Outstanding checks $620.
   - Bank service charge $18.
   - Note collected by bank $1300.
   - Deposit in transit $430.

   B. Prepare the entries necessary to correct the ledger accounts affected by these transactions.

   C. After the entries in (B), above, have been posted, what is the balance in the Cash account?

Connamara Marble Co.
Bank Reconciliation
December 31, 19__

Book balance	$	Bank balance	$
ADD:		ADD:	
DEDUCT:		DEDUCT:	

3. Transactions for the Zayas Corp. pertaining to petty cash were as follows:

February	2	Established a $100 petty cash fund.
March	5	Replenished the fund. Cash remaining was $17 and petty cash receipts were for office supplies, $27; delivery charges, $31; transportation expense, $19; and miscellaneous expense, $6.
March	5	Since the fund did not last as long as expected, it was decided to increase the maximum balance to $150.

What are the general journal entries necessary to establish and maintain the fund?

8

PROMISSORY NOTES

OBJECTIVES

After completing this chapter, you should be able to:

- Calculate the simple interest and maturity value of a loan.
- Explain the difference between an interest-bearing promissory note and non-interest-bearing note.
- Identify the various parts of a promissory note.

If you live in an apartment, you use the property of the landlord and pay a price (rent) for the use of the property. On the other hand, if you live in a house that you own, you probably borrowed most of the purchase price from the bank. This borrowed money also commands a price, called *interest*. In a sense, you are renting this money from the lending institution and interest is the rent on the property.

Interest—The price paid for the use of someone else's money.

CALCULATING SIMPLE INTEREST

There are three factors which determine how much interest will be paid when money is borrowed.

1. *Principal:* This is the amount of money borrowed. If everything else is equal, a person who borrows $2000 will have to pay more interest than the person who borrows $1000.
2. *Rate:* This is the price of the loan expressed as a percentage of the amount borrowed. It is always quoted on a yearly basis, but, as we will see, it is adjusted for the actual length of time the money is borrowed. A person who borrows $1000 for a year at a 12% rate will pay $120 in interest, whereas one who borrows the $1000 for a year at a 10% rate will pay $100.
3. *Time:* This is the number of days, months, and years for which the money has been borrowed. This factor also determines how much a person will pay in interest. Clearly, a person who borrows $1000 for a year at 12% rate must pay more than one who borrows the same money for only one month.

When calculating interest, we use the three preceding factors in this formula:

$$I = PRT$$

where: I = Interest
P = Principal
R = Rate
T = Time

A second formula is used to determine the maturity value (MV) of the loan:

$$MV = P + I$$

Maturity Value—the total amount of money that must be paid back at the end of the loan period. It is equal to the original amount borrowed (principal) plus the interest charge.

We will now develop a model for the calculation of interest which will be usable in all of our problems.

$$\text{Interest} = \text{Principal} \times \text{Rate} \times \text{Time}$$

$$I = \frac{\text{Principal}}{1} \times \frac{\text{Rate}}{100} \times \frac{\text{Exact days}}{360}$$

Notice that the denominators remain constant regardless of the problem. Actually, the time factor can be calculated in three other ways, each producing a slightly different interest charge. The fraction we are using, exact days/360, is the one most frequently used by banks and other financial institutions.

Example: A manufacturer borrows $6000 from the Second National Bank for 120 days. The bank charges a 12% rate of interest. How much interest will the bank charge on this loan and what is the maturity value?

$$I = PRT$$

$$I = \frac{6000}{1} \times \frac{12}{100} \times \frac{120}{360}$$

$$I = \frac{\overset{60}{6000}}{1} \quad \frac{\overset{4}{12}}{\underset{1}{100}} \quad \frac{\overset{1}{120}}{\underset{\underset{1}{3}}{360}}$$

Reduce by Cancellation

$$I = \frac{240}{1} = \$240$$

$MV = P + I$
$MV = 6000 + 240$
$MV = \$6240$

The bank will charge $240 interest and the manufacturer will pay the bank $6240 at maturity.

PROMISSORY NOTES

A negotiable promissory note is an unconditional written promise, made by one person to another and signed by the maker, agreeing to pay a definite sum of money on demand or at a specified future date.

$3000 Scarsdale, New York April 11, 19--

Sixty days AFTER DATE I PROMISE TO PAY

TO THE ORDER OF Michael Amoroso

Three thousand and No/100 DOLLARS

FOR VALUE RECEIVED WITH INTEREST AT 10%

PAYABLE AT FIRST NATIONAL BANK OF SCARSDALE

DUE June 10, 19-- Robert Grippo

Figure 8-1. Interest-Bearing Promissory Note

In this promissory note, we see that Robert Grippo (the maker) has unconditionally promised to pay Michael Amoroso (the payee) a definite sum of money ($3000 plus interest for 60 days at 10%) at a specified future date (June 10, 19__).

Using the formulas you have just learned, calculate the interest on this note and also the maturity value.

$$I = PRT$$

$$I = \frac{3000}{1} \times \frac{10}{100} \times \frac{60}{360}$$

$$I = \$50$$

$$MV = P + I$$
$$MV = \$3000 + \$50$$
$$MV = \$3050$$

We will now look at a second promissory note; this one is almost identical to Figure 8-1 except for one piece of information. Can you find the difference?

$3000 Scarsdale, New York April 11, 19--

Sixty days AFTER DATE I PROMISE TO PAY

TO THE ORDER OF Michael Amoroso

Three thousand and No/100 DOLLARS

FOR VALUE RECEIVED

PAYABLE AT First National Bank of Scarsdale

DUE June 10, 19-- Robert Grippo

Figure 8-2. Non-Interest-Bearing Note

The difference is that Figure 8-2 contains no information about the rate of interest charged. Does this mean that the lender charged no interest on the second loan? No, it is unlikely, given the high cost of money, that one person will lend $3000 to another without interest unless that person is a relative or close friend. It is most probable that in this situation the interest was deducted *in advance*, and therefore the interest rate does not have to be recorded on the face of the instrument.

Here is a problem which will help you to distinguish the differences between the two types of notes. Let us imagine that you are looking for a $2000 loan for 90 days, but you decide to compare the rates charged by two local banks before arriving at a decision. Bank A agrees to lend the $2000 for 90 days at a rate of 12 percent. What is the interest and maturity value on this loan?

$$I = PRT$$

$$I = \frac{2000}{1} \times \frac{12}{100} \times \frac{90}{360}$$

$$I = \$60$$

$$MV = P + I$$
$$MV = 2000 + 60$$
$$MV = \$2060$$

Bank A will lend you $2000 now and you are required to pay them $2060 at end of 90 days. Your liability would be evidenced by a note similar to Figure 8-1 (interest-bearing), on which the interest rate would be specified.

Now assume that you walk across the street to Bank B which also quotes a 12% rate but deducts the interest in advance. The interest charge will still be $60 since the rate (12%) is the same as Bank A. The only difference is that they will deduct the $60 at the time the loan is made, leaving you with $1940. When you repay the loan you must pay them $2000. In this situation, there is no need for the interest rate to appear on the face of the note since it was deducted at the time of loan. This is how the so-called non-interest-bearing note usually originates. As you can see, this name can be misleading since in most cases an interest charge has been made.

By the way, given a choice of Bank A or Bank B which would you choose and why?

Bank A offers the better terms. In each case, you are paying $60 interest, but Bank A lends you the entire $2000, whereas Bank B only lends you $1940. Therefore, you get more for your money from Bank A. Notice that you are not charged twice by Bank B. The difference between what you walk out of the bank with ($1940) and what you repay ($2000) is still $60.

PROBLEMS

(Answers on page 112)

$10000 Valhalla, Oklahoma May 19, 19--

Ninety days AFTER DATE We PROMISE TO PAY

TO THE ORDER OF Wallace Lumber Co.

Ten thousand and No/100 DOLLARS

FOR VALUE RECEIVED WITH INTEREST AT 12%

PAYABLE AT Valhalla National Bank

DUE August 17, 19--

Charles Calhoun

Carol Calhoun

1. Refer to the promissory note above and identify the following parts:

- **a.** Payee
- **b.** Maker
- **c.** Date of the note
- **d.** Maturity date
- **e.** Principal
- **f.** Rate
- **g.** Time

2. Again referring to the above note, calculate the interest on the note and its maturity value.

9

ENTRIES FOR PROMISSORY NOTES

OBJECTIVES

After completing this chapter, you should be able to:

- Prepare journal entries to record the issuance and payment of promissory notes.
- Recognize the differences in recording interest-bearing and discounted notes.
- Prepare the journal entry needed to record a dishonored note.

NOTES PAYABLE AND INTEREST EXPENSE

Whenever a person or company issues a note payable, both a liability and an expense are created on the books of the maker. The liability (notes payable) is created immediately, while the expense (interest expense) builds up over the length of the loan.

Interest-Bearing Notes Payable

Promissory notes are most often issued for the following purposes:

1. Borrow money from a bank.
2. Make purchases.
3. Obtain a time extension on a debt.

Journal entries for these three situations follow. In each transaction, an interest-bearing note was issued and payment made on the maturity date. You should verify the interest charge in each transaction in order to develop a facility with these calculations.

Example 1—NOTE ISSUED TO BANK

On June 14, Ken Brown borrowed $6000 for 60 days at a 13% interest rate.

Issuance of note:

June 14	Cash	6,000	
	Notes Payable		6,000

Payment of note:

August 13	Notes Payable	6,000	
	Interest Expense	130	
	Cash		6,130

Example 2—NOTE ISSUED FOR PLANT AND EQUIPMENT

On September 27, the Toledo Co. purchases a $15,000 cutting machine by paying $5000 cash and issuing a $10,000, 30-day, 12% note.

Issuance of note:

Sept. 27	Machinery	15000 –	
	Cash		5000 –
	Notes Payable		10000 –

Payment of note:

Oct. 27	Notes Payable	10000 –	
	Interest Expense	100 –	
	Cash		10100 –

Example 3—EXTENSION OF AN EXISTING LIABILITY

On May 12, the Buffalo Co. could not pay the $1500 account payable owed to the Pacific Corp. due this date. The Buffalo Co. asked for and was granted a 30-day extension. However, the Buffalo Co. must now issue a promissory note and pay interest at an 8% rate. Notice that the note payable replaces the account payable.

Issuance of note:

May 12	Accounts Payable-Pacific Corp.	1500 –	
	Notes Payable		1500 –

Payment of note:

June 11	Notes Payable	1500 –	
	Interest Expense	10 –	
	Cash		1510 –

Non-Interest-Bearing Notes Payable

Earlier, we saw that in some situations the interest is deducted at the time the loan is made. This is known as discounting a note. The only change that occurs in the journal entries is that the interest expense is recorded when payment is made. Technically speaking, this entry is premature because there is no interest expense when the note is issued. Interest expense builds up over the life of the loan. We will ignore this fact because eventually all of the interest will become an expense.

Example 4—NOTE DISCOUNTED BY A BANK

On December 3, Steve Melnyk borrowed $9000 for 120 days at a 10% interest rate.

Issuance of note:

Date	Account	Debit	Credit
Dec. 3	Cash	8700—	
	Interest Expense	300—	
	Notes Payable		9000—

Payment of Note:

Date	Account	Debit	Credit
April 2	Notes Payable	9000—	
	Cash		9000—

NOTES RECEIVABLE AND INTEREST INCOME

Thus far, we have concentrated our efforts on the analysis of notes payable. However, what is a note payable to one company becomes a note receivable to another, and what is interest expense to the debtor is interest income to the creditor.

Interest-Bearing Notes Receivable

In each of the following situations we will use a transaction previously analyzed from the point of view of the maker of the note, only this time we will record the journal entries as they appear on the books of the creditor.

Example 5—INTEREST-BEARING NOTE HELD BY BANK

On June 14, Ken Brown borrowed $6000 for 60 days at a 13% interest rate (see *Example 1*).

Issuance of note:

Date	Account	Debit	Credit
June 14	Notes Receivable	6000 —	
	Cash		6000 —

Payment of note:

Date	Account	Debit	Credit
Aug 13	Cash	6130 —	
	Notes Receivable		6000 —
	Interest Income		130 —

Example 6—NOTE ISSUED FOR PLANT AND EQUIPMENT

On September 27, the Toledo Co. purchased a $15,000 cutting machine by paying $5000 cash and issuing a $10,000, 30-day, 12% note (see *Example 2*).

Issuance of note:

Date	Account	Debit	Credit
Sept. 27	Cash	5000 —	
	Notes Receivable	10000 —	
	Sales		15000 —

Payment of note:

Date	Account	Debit	Credit
Oct. 27	Cash	10100 —	
	Notes Receivable		10000 —
	Interest Income		100 —

Example 7—EXTENSION OF AN EXISTING LIABILITY

On May 12, the Buffalo Co. could not pay the $1500 account payable owed to the Pacific Corp. due this date. The Buffalo Co. asked for and was granted a 30-day extension, but was required to sign a promissory note and pay interest at an 8% rate (See *Example 3*).

Issuance of note:

Date	Account	Debit	Credit
May 12	Notes Receivable	1500 —	
	Accounts Receivable-Buffalo Co.		1500 —

Payment of note:

June 11	Cash		1510—	
	Notes Receivable			1500—
	Interest Income			10—

Non-Interest-Bearing Notes Receivable

We know that when a note is discounted the interest is deducted in advance. The creditor or holder of the note records the interest charge as interest income upon receipt of the note. Once again, for the sake of simplicity, we will ignore the fact that the total interest does not become interest income until the note matures.

Example 8—NOTE DISCOUNTED BY A BANK

On December 3, Steve Melnyk borrowed $9000 for 120 days at a 10% interest rate. The bank deducted the interest in advance (see *Example 4*).

Issuance of note:

Dec. 3	Notes Receivable		9000—	
	Cash			8700—
	Interest Income			300—

Payment of note:

April 2	Cash		9000—	
	Notes Receivable			9000—

DISHONORED NOTES RECEIVABLE

A note is dishonored when the maker cannot make payment on the maturity date. When this happens, the principal in the Notes Receivable account and the interest in the Interest Income account are transferred to Accounts Receivable. If this procedure is followed, the Notes Receivable account will show only the amount of notes that have not matured. Another advantage of the transfer is that if the maker of the dishonored note applies for credit again, the account will reveal that payment is due on the principal and interest.

To illustrate this entry, let us assume the Commodore Corp. holds a $2000, 9%, 80-day note of William Hynes. The note was dishonored at maturity and Commodore made the following entry:

Date		Account	Debit	Credit
Aug.	3	Accounts Receivable-William Hynes	2040—	
		Notes Receivable		2000—
		Interest Income		40—

Notice that the Interest Income account receives a credit to transfer the interest earned to Accounts Receivable. In spite of the fact that it has not been collected, the interest has been earned and is still part of the total debt owed by William Hynes.

PROBLEMS

(Answers on page 112)

1. Prepare general journal entries to record the following transactions for the Drummond Corp.

June	8	Purchased $7000 of merchandise from the Arnaiz Co. by issuing a 30-day, 12% promissory note.
	11	Borrowed $10,000 from the Bank of Southport for 45 days at a 12% rate. The bank deducted the interest in advance.
	17	Requested and received an extension on a $2000 account payable due this date. Issued a 60-day, 15% promissory note to the Spellman Co. in settlement of the open account.
July	8	Paid the amount due the Arnaiz Co.
	26	Paid the amount due the Bank of Southport.
Aug.	16	Paid the amount due the Spellman Co.

2. Using the transactions in Problem 1, prepare general journal entries as they would appear on the books of the *holder* of the note. (For example, how would the Arnaiz Co. record the entry of June 8?)

10

DISCOUNTING NOTES RECEIVABLE

OBJECTIVES

After completing this chapter, you should be able to:

- Describe the procedures involved in discounting notes receivable.
- Calculate the cash proceeds of a discounted note.
- Prepare general journal entries to record the discounting of a note receivable and its payment by the maker.
- Prepare general journal entries to record the dishonor of a discounted note and its subsequent collection.

THE PURPOSE OF DISCOUNTING

Many business firms experience wide seasonal fluctuations in the amount of cash they have available to pay bills. When the balance swings to a low level, the firm may decide to convert their notes receivable to cash by discounting them to maturity. The bank pays cash for the note, less a charge or discount. If the maker of the note fails to pay the maturity value when it is due, the firm discounting the note must reimburse the bank. The discounting firm therefore has a *contingent liability* to the bank. It is a liability which may or may not arise, depending on the actions of the maker of the note.

CALCULATING THE PROCEEDS OF THE NOTE

Before we think about recording the journal entries for discounted notes receivable, we must devote some time to the calculation of the proceeds of the note. The proceeds consist of the cash total received from the bank when the note receivable is sold. The following steps are necessary to compute the proceeds of a discounted note:

1. *Determine the maturity value of the note.* We have done this before. Recall the two formulas:
   a. I = PRT (Interest = Principal × Rate × Time)
   b. MV = P + I (Maturity Value = Principal + Interest)
2. *Find the discount period.* This is the length of time the bank will hold the note. The bank charge (discount) is based in part on the length of the discount period. If everything else is equal, the longer the bank holds the note, the higher the discount charge will be. Specifically, the discount period is the number of days running from the day the note is discounted to the maturity date, when the maker pays the bank.
3. *Calculate the bank discount.* This is the fee charged by a bank for performing the discounting function. On the discount date, the bank lends the company the maturity value of the note and deducts the interest charge (discount) in advance from the maturity value. Since this is a loan, we must go back to the basic terms of principal, rate, and time in order to compute the interest charge. The actual calculation is identical to the method used to determine the interest charge (I = P × R × T). The terms,however, are different. The discount equals the maturity value times the discount rate times the discount period (D = MV × DR × DP).

   D = Discount = Interest charged by the bank for discounting the note. It is equivalent to the calculation of I (Interest) in our original formula.
   MV = Maturity Value = The amount the maker of the note has agreed to pay and the bank expects to collect on the maturity date. As used here, it is equivalent to P (Principal) in the original formula.
   DR = Discount Rate = The rate of interest charged by the bank when discounting the note. It is important to remember that this is different from the rate of interest on the note used to determine the maturity value. The bank determines what this rate will be. It had no control over the rate of interest charged on the note. For purposes of calculating the discount, DR is used in the same way that R (Rate) was used to compute interest.
   DP = Discount Period = The length of time the bank holds the note. It is used in the same manner that T (time) was used in our original formula.
4. *Determine the cash proceeds.* The cash proceeds (CP) is determined by subtracting the discount (D) from the maturity value (MV).

$$CP = MV - D$$

or

$$CP = MV - (MV \times DR \times DP)$$

We will now use the last formula to calculate the proceeds of a discounted note receivable.

Problem: Panella Furniture Co. was the payee of a $4000, 90-day note dated August 10, with interest at 12%. The note was given by the Vasti Corp. to obtain a time extension on an open account debt. On September 9, 60 days prior to maturity, Panella Furniture Co. discounted the note at their bank at 15%.

a. What is the maturity value of the note?
b. How much did the Panella Furniture Co. receive (cash proceeds) from the sale of the note?
c. How much interest did Panella Furniture earn on the note?

Analysis: We will use the following time line to help us trace the sequence of events in the problem. You should draw one for every problem. It does not have to be as elaborate as this; even a simple model will be very useful.

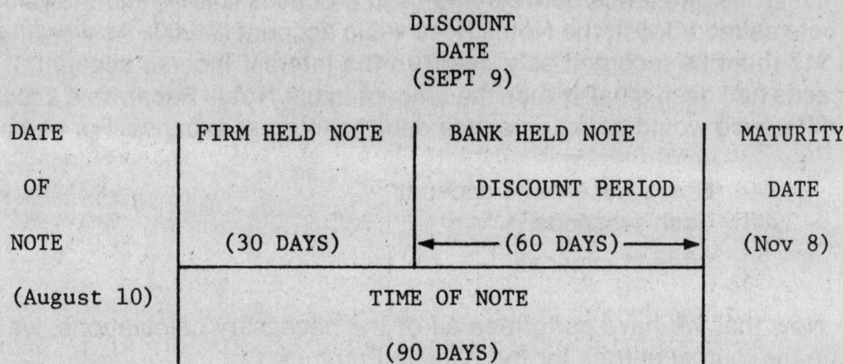

Part a. In order to calculate the maturity value, we must use the formulas I = PRT and MV = P + I:

$$I = PRT$$

$$I = \frac{4000}{1} \times \frac{12}{100} \times \frac{90}{360}$$

$$I = \$120$$

$$MV = P + I$$
$$MV = \$4000 + \$120$$
$$MV = \$4120$$

The maturity value of the note is $4120. Whoever holds this instrument on the maturity date expects to collect this amount from the maker.

Part b. The cash proceeds can be determined by using the formula CP = MV − (MV × DR × DP). The individual terms are:

MV = Maturity Value = $4120
DR = Discount Rate = 15%
DP = Discount Period = 60 days

Therefore:

$$CP = MV - (MV \times DR \times DP)$$

$$CP = \$4120 - \left(\frac{4120}{1} \times \frac{15}{100} \times \frac{60}{360}\right)$$

$$CP = \$4120 - \$103$$
$$CP = \$4017$$

On Sept. 9, the discount date, the Panella Furniture Co. received $4017 from the sale of the note receivable. The bank will hold the note until the maturity date and receive the maturity value ($4120) from the maker. The difference between the maturity value and the amount given to Panella Furniture is the bank's profit, which we know is $103. If, for some reason, the maker does not pay the note on the maturity date, the Panella Co. must pay the *maturity value* to the bank and attempt to collect the money from the maker.

Part **c**. The Panella Furniture Co. earned $17 on this note. This is determined by finding the difference between the cash proceeds ($4017) and the value of the note as recorded in the Notes Receivable account ($4000). As we will see, this $17 must be recorded as a credit to the Interest Income account. If the proceeds had been smaller than the amount in the Notes Receivable account, the difference would be entered as a debit to interest expense. For example:

$4000	Notes Receivable account
–3980	Cash proceeds
$ 20	Interest expense

Now that we have performed all of the necessary calculations, we will create the journal entries for the Panella Furniture Co.

NOTE PAID BY MAKER

On August 10, Panella Furniture accepted the note and granted a time extension on the $4000 debt owed by the Vasti Corp.

Date	Account	Debit	Credit
Aug. 10	Notes Receivable	4000	
	Accounts Receivable-Vasti Corp.		4000–

On September 9, Panella Furniture discounted the promissory note at the bank.

Date	Account	Debit	Credit
Sept 9	Cash	4017–	
	Notes Receivable Discounted		4000–
	Interest Income		17–

Notice that the credit was not to the Notes Receivable account but to an account called Notes Receivable Discounted. We do this because the company has a contingent liability to the bank and we do not want to remove the $4000 from the Notes Receivable account until the liability is eliminated.

In this situation, we will assume that the maker paid the bank on the maturity date, which relieved the Panella Co. of any liability to the bank.

The note receivable and contingent liability can now be removed from the accounts.

Date	Account	Debit	Credit
Nov. 8	Notes Receivable Discounted	4000—	
	Notes Receivable		4000—

NOTE DISHONORED BY MAKER

If the Vasti Corp. dishonors the note on the maturity date, the bank will seek payment from Panella Furniture. When this happens, the contingent liability becomes an actual liability and the bank must be paid the maturity value. Two journal entries are required. The first is identical to that recorded when the maker pays the note. It removes the contingent liability and the note receivable from the accounts.

Date	Account	Debit	Credit
Nov. 8	Notes Receivable Discounted	4000-	
	Notes Receivable		4000—

The second entry reduces the Cash account by the amount of the maturity value and transfers this amount to accounts receivable. This is the same procedure we used previously when the maker defaulted on a note payable to the payee.

Date	Account	Debit	Credit
Nov. 8	Accounts Receivable - Vasti Corp.	4120-	
	Cash		4120-

COLLECTING A DISHONORED NOTE

Panella Furniture has paid the bank $4120, transferred this amount to accounts receivable, and will now attempt to collect the debt from Vasti Corp. In addition to the maturity value, they will also seek to collect interest on the debt from the maturity date to the date of collection.

If Panella Furniture collects the debt on Oct. 8, they are entitled to collect 30 days' interest on the maturity value and record it as interest income. Let us assume that the interest rate charged for this 30-day period is 12%, which is the same rate used in the original note. The interest calculation is:

$$I = PRT$$

$$I = \frac{4120}{1} \times \frac{12}{100} \times \frac{30}{360}$$

$$I = \$41.20$$

The journal entry on the collection date is:

Date	Account	Debit	Credit
Oct. 8	Cash	4161 20	
	Accounts Receivable - Vasti Corp.		4120 —
	Interest Income		41 20

In the next chapter, we will discover what happens when a debt becomes uncollectable and must be removed from the accounts.

PROBLEMS

(Answers on page 113)

1. On April 20, the Short Co. accepted a $2000, 90-day, 16% note from Mary Green in granting a time extension on her past-due account. On June 19, 30 days prior to maturity, the Short Co. discounted the note receivable at their bank at a discount rate of 15%. On July 19, the maturity date, Mary Green dishonored the note. Thirty days beyond maturity, August 18, Mary Green paid the maturity value plus 30 days' interest at 16%.

- **a.** What is the maturity value of the note?
- **b.** What were the cash proceeds of the discounted note?
- **c.** How much interest did the Short Co. earn on the note when it was discounted?

2. Using the information contained in the preceding problem, create general journal entries for the following dates:

- **a.** April 20, the date of the note.
- **b.** June 19, the discount date.
- **c.** July 19, the maturity date.
- **d.** August 18, the collection date.

11

WRITING OFF AN UNCOLLECTABLE ACCOUNT

OBJECTIVES

After completing this chapter, you should be able to:

- Explain the difference between the direct method and the allowance method of writing off an uncollectable account.
- Prepare journal entries to record the write-off and subsequent collection of a debt using the direct write-off method.
- Prepare journal entries to record the estimation, write-off, and recovery of bad debts using the allowance method.

DIRECT WRITE-OFF METHOD

Each time a firm extends credit to a customer, it exposes itself to the risk that the debt will never be repaid. The company could ensure that all debts will be repaid by selling only to its most credit-worthy customers. However, if this were done, they would lose the profits that would have been generated from sales to the excluded customers. Faced with this dilemma, most companies try to arrive at a balance between bad debts and lost sales.

When a debt becomes uncollectable, two events must take place:

1. An asset account must be reduced by the amount of the bad debt. This account is always Accounts Receivable. Recall that even when a note was dishonored by the maker, the maturity value was transferred from the Notes Receivable account to Accounts Receivable. All write-offs of bad debts are made from Accounts Receivable.
2. An expense account must be increased. We know that a business expense is a cost incurred in generating sales revenue. All uncollectable debts arise from the extension of credit to a customer at the time of sale. The name of the expense account is, logically, Bad

Debts Expense and, like all other expenses, appears in the expense section of the income statement.

The journal entry for writing off an $800 uncollectable account of P. Ruppert is:

Date	Account	Debit	Credit
May 21	Bad Debts Expense	800—	
	Accounts Receivable-P. Ruppert		800—

If, at some later date, the company collects the account written off, two entries are needed to correct the accounting records.

1. The first entry reinstates the customer's account. Notice that is a reversal of the write-off entry of May 21.

Date	Account	Debit	Credit
Sept 15	Accounts Receivable-P. Ruppert	800—	
	Bad Debts Expense		800—

2. The second entry records the payment by the customer. It is no different from the entry that would have been recorded if he had paid on time.

Date	Account	Debit	Credit
Sept 15	Cash	800—	
	Accounts Receivable-P. Ruppert		800—

There are certain theoretical objections to the procedures we have just used to write-off a bad debt. This method should be used only in situations where bad debt losses are small in relation to total sales and net income. We will explore this problem further in the next section and develop a more appropriate method for handling uncollectable accounts.

ALLOWANCE METHOD

In the calculation of net income, one of the most fundamental principles of accounting is that *revenue must be matched with the expenses incurred in generating that revenue*. It is this *matching principle* that makes the direct write-off method unacceptable except in certain situations. Bad debts expense arises from the selling of goods on credit to customers who fail to pay their bills. Therefore, a bad debt expense should appear on the same income statement that contains the sale which gave rise to the bad debt. If a sale takes place in one year and is written off as a bad debt the next year, the matching principle is violated. This can happen when the direct write-off method is used.

At this point, a logical predicament arises. If we are preparing an income statement on December 31, how can we predict which of the sales made in the past year will become bad debts in the future? Since this is obviously impossible, we must use an *estimated* amount of bad debts expense for the past year.

Estimating Uncollectable Accounts

Any estimate is based on the firm's historical experience with bad debt losses. For instance, when a company has experienced bad debt losses of one half of 1% of credit sales, it assumes that this rate is applicable to the past year's credit sales. If the company is preparing the year-end financial statements and has $800,000 of credit sales, it calculates that $4000 will be uncollectable ($800,000 × .005 = $4000). The general journal entry would be:

Date	Account	Debit	Credit
Dec 31	Bad Debts Expense	4000—	
	Allowance for Uncollectable Accounts		4000—

Bad Debts Expense appears in the expense section of the income statement and the Allowance account is found in the asset section of the balance sheet as a subtraction from accounts receivable. The Allowance account is a contra account to accounts receivable. Since it is estimated that $4000 of the accounts receivable will be uncollectable, accounts receivable should be reported on the balance sheet as a net amount. If the Accounts Receivable account has a $70,000 debit balance, it would be reported on the balance sheet as:

	Accounts Receivable	$70000—	
	Less: Allowance for Uncollectable Accts.	4000—	$66000—

The $66,000 is the estimated collectable value of the accounts receivable on that date.

Writing Off a Bad Debt

Whenever an account is considered to be uncollectable, it is written off against the Allowance account. This account has a $4000 credit balance which will decline every time an account is charged against it. Let us assume that on January 24 the $600 account of L. Coldrick is deemed to be uncollectable. The appropriate journal entry is:

Date	Account	Debit	Credit
Jan. 24	Allowance for Uncollectable Accounts	600—	
	Accounts Receivable–L. Coldrick		600—

This entry has the effect of removing the $600 from the Accounts Receivable controlling account and the subsidiary account. It also reduces the Allowance account to a balance of $3400.

GENERAL LEDGER

Accounts Receivable	
(BAL) 7000—	(1/24) 600—

Allowance for Uncollectable Accounts	
(1/24) 600—	(BAL) 4000—

ACCOUNTS RECEIVABLE LEDGER

L. Coldrick	
(BAL) 600—	(1/24) 600—

Notice the effect this transaction has on the balance sheet. Although the balances in both the Accounts Receivable and the Allowance account have changed, the net amount of accounts receivable has remained the same.

Accounts Receivable	$69,400	
Less: Allowance for Uncollectable Accounts	3,400	$66,000

Bad Debt Recoveries

The customer who had his account written off as uncollectable may attempt to restore his previous credit standing by paying the debt at a later date. In order to show, in the individual account, that payment has been made, it is necessary to record two journal entries. The first reinstates the Accounts Receivable account and the second records the receipt of cash.

1. Reinstate the Account

Date	Account	Debit	Credit
Apr. 3	Accounts Receivable–L. Coldrick	600—	
	Allowance for Uncollectable Accounts		600—

2. Record Receipt of Cash

Apr. 3	Cash	600—	
	Accounts Receivable-L. Coldrick		600—

PROBLEMS

(Answers on page 114)

1. Raleigh Motor Sales uses the direct method of writing off bad debts. On June 14, Raleigh determined that an $1100 debt owed by Tom Carty was uncollectable and wrote it off. In an attempt to reestablish his previous credit standing, Mr. Carty paid his debt on Nov. 17.

Using the direct method, prepare journal entries to record:

a. the write-off of the debt
b. the recovery of the debt

2. Carroll Corp. is preparing year-end financial statements on Dec. 31 and estimates bad debt losses to be one-half of 1% of its credit sales of $500,000. Three weeks later, on Jan. 21, Carroll Corp. wrote off the $400 uncollectable account of F. Farbent. On May 19, Mr. Farbent paid the debt in full.

Using the allowance method, prepare journal entries to record:

a. the year-end estimation
b. the write-off of Jan. 21
c. the May 19 debt recovery

12

PAYROLL SYSTEMS

OBJECTIVES

After completing this chapter, you should be able to:

- Describe the payroll taxes withheld from employee paychecks.
- Describe the payroll taxes levied directly on the employer.
- Prepare a payroll register.
- Create a general journal entry to record the information contained in the payroll register.
- Prepare a general journal entry to record payroll taxes levied on the employer.

INTRODUCTION TO THE PAYROLL

Many people are interested in the preparation of the payroll. The employee has a natural curiosity in how his check is prepared. The employer has a strong interest in the payroll for three reasons:

1. Labor costs are a major expense in many businesses.
2. Employers must comply with a complex variety of federal, state, and local regulations governing payroll taxes.
3. Employees expect that payroll checks will be calculated accurately, paid promptly, and supported with a detailed explanation of deductions.

This chapter will focus first on the calculations and legal requirements applicable to payroll accounting and then on the general journal entries needed to record the payroll and related taxes.

CALCULATING GROSS PAY

The starting point in calculating a payroll check is the *gross pay*. Every employee knows well that the take-home pay is always less than the amount earned.

NET PAY = GROSS PAY – DEDUCTIONS

Gross pay, for one employee may be a salary or fixed amount of money each payroll period. For example, the employee may receive a salary of $3000 per month. Overtime work does not increase this employee's gross pay. On the other hand, an employee may be paid on a wage basis, such as a specific rate of pay for each hour worked. A person paid an hourly rate received overtime pay for all work in excess of the standard work week, usually forty hours. Frequently, the overtime rate per hour is 150% ("time and a half") of the regular hourly rate.

The following formula can be used to calculate an employee's gross pay if the person is paid on an hourly basis:

$$GP = (40 \times R) + 1.5R\,(H - 40)$$

where: GP = Gross Pay
R = Regular Rate per Hour
H = Total Hours Worked

Example: Quentin Fiorello is paid $6 per hour for a standard 40-hour work week. Overtime pay is calculated using 150% of the regular hourly rate. Find his gross pay for a week in which he worked 48 hours.

$GP = (40 \times R) + 1.5R\,(H - 40)$
$GP = (40 \times \$6) + 1.5 \text{ X } \$6\,(48 - 40)$
$GP = \$240 + \$9\,(8)$
$GP = \$240 + \$72$
$GP = \$312$

EMPLOYEE PAYROLL DEDUCTIONS

Payroll deductions are subtracted from the gross pay to arrive at the *net pay*. Many of the deductions are required by law, while others are authorized by the employee. Regardless of the deductions, the business is acting only as a collection agent. Ultimately, all collected money must be turned over to governmental or private agencies.

Social Security (FICA) Taxes

The Federal Insurance Contributions Act (FICA) stipulates that employers are required to withhold a portion of each employee's earnings as a contribution to the Social Security program. An additional contribution, equal to the employee's must be paid by the employer. If the employee has $70 deducted for social security, the employer is required to match this with another $70 contribution to the employee's account.

The FICA tax helps pay benefits to retirees, disabled persons and dependents of deceased workers. Under the Medicare portion of the program, it also provides health insurance for those age 65 and over.

Federal and State Income Taxes

In addition to FICA, employers are required to withhold funds for the payment of the employee's income taxes. The amount ot tax withheld depends on the employee's taxable wages, marital status, number of dependents claimed, and the frequency of payroll periods.

MARRIED Persons—**WEEKLY** Payroll Period

(For Wages Paid After June 1982 and Before July 1983)

And the wages are—		And the number of withholding allowances claimed is—										
At least	But less than	0	1	2	3	4	5	6	7	8	9	10 or more
		The amount of income tax to be withheld shall be—										
$310	$320	$42.70	$39.10	$35.40	$31.80	$28.10	$24.80	$21.70	$18.70	$15.60	$12.50	$9.40
320	330	44.60	41.00	37.30	33.70	30.00	26.40	23.30	20.30	17.20	14.10	11.00
330	340	46.50	42.90	39.20	35.60	31.90	28.30	24.90	21.90	18.80	15.70	12.60
340	350	48.40	44.80	41.10	37.50	33.80	30.20	26.50	23.50	20.40	17.30	14.20
350	360	50.30	46.70	43.00	39.40	35.70	32.10	28.40	25.10	22.00	18.90	15.80
360	370	52.70	48.60	44.90	41.30	37.60	34.00	30.30	26.70	23.60	20.50	17.40
370	380	55.10	50.50	46.80	43.20	39.50	35.90	32.20	28.60	25.20	22.10	19.00
380	390	57.50	52.80	48.70	45.10	41.40	37.80	34.10	30.50	26.80	23.70	20.60
390	400	59.90	55.20	50.60	47.00	43.30	39.70	36.00	32.40	28.70	25.30	22.20
400	410	62.30	57.60	53.00	48.90	45.20	41.60	37.90	34.30	30.60	26.90	23.80
410	420	64.70	60.00	55.40	50.80	47.10	43.50	39.80	36.20	32.50	28.80	25.40
420	430	67.10	62.40	57.80	53.20	49.00	45.40	41.70	38.10	34.40	30.70	27.10
430	440	69.50	64.80	60.20	55.60	51.00	47.30	43.60	40.00	36.30	32.60	29.00
440	450	71.90	67.20	62.60	58.00	53.40	49.20	45.50	41.90	38.20	34.50	30.90
450	460	74.30	69.60	65.00	60.40	55.80	51.20	47.40	43.80	40.10	36.40	32.80
460	470	77.00	72.00	67.40	62.80	58.20	53.60	49.30	45.70	42.00	38.30	34.70
470	480	79.70	74.50	69.80	65.20	60.60	56.00	51.40	47.60	43.90	40.20	36.60
480	490	82.40	77.20	72.20	67.60	63.00	58.40	53.80	49.50	45.80	42.10	38.50
490	500	85.10	79.90	74.70	70.00	65.40	60.80	56.20	51.60	47.70	44.00	40.40
500	510	87.80	82.60	77.40	72.40	67.80	63.20	58.60	54.00	49.60	45.90	42.30
510	520	90.50	85.30	80.10	74.90	70.20	65.60	61.00	56.40	51.70	47.80	44.20
520	530	93.20	88.00	82.80	77.60	72.60	68.00	63.40	58.80	54.10	49.70	46.10
530	540	95.90	90.70	85.50	80.30	75.10	70.40	65.80	61.20	56.50	51.90	48.00
540	550	98.60	93.40	88.20	83.00	77.80	72.80	68.20	63.60	58.90	54.30	49.90
550	560	101.30	96.10	90.90	85.70	80.50	75.30	70.60	66.00	61.30	56.70	52.10
560	570	104.50	98.80	93.60	88.40	83.20	78.00	73.00	68.40	63.70	59.10	54.50
570	580	107.70	101.50	96.30	91.10	85.90	80.70	75.50	70.80	66.10	61.50	56.90
580	590	110.90	104.70	99.00	93.80	88.60	83.40	78.20	73.20	68.50	63.90	59.30
590	600	114.10	107.90	101.70	96.50	91.30	86.10	80.90	75.70	70.90	66.30	61.70
600	610	117.30	111.10	104.90	99.20	94.00	88.80	83.60	78.40	73.30	68.70	64.10
610	620	120.50	114.30	108.10	102.00	96.70	91.50	86.30	81.10	76.00	71.10	66.50
620	630	123.70	117.50	111.30	105.20	99.40	94.20	89.00	83.80	78.70	73.50	68.90
630	640	126.90	120.70	114.50	108.40	102.20	96.90	91.70	86.50	81.40	76.20	71.30
640	650	130.10	123.90	117.70	111.60	105.40	99.60	94.40	89.20	84.10	78.90	73.70
650	660	133.30	127.10	120.90	114.80	108.60	102.50	97.10	91.90	86.80	81.60	76.40

Figure 12-1. Wage Bracket Withholding Table

The Internal Revenue Service provides withholding tables for different payroll periods. An example of a *wage bracket withholding table* is shown in Figure 12-1. This table would be used for married employees who receive a weekly paycheck.

Example: James Wray, who is married and claims 8 exemptions, earned a gross pay of $617.32 in the week ended May 4. What is the amount of federal income taxes his employer should withhold?

The employer would move down the left side of the table (Figure 12-1) to the line that reads "at least $610 but less that $620." Next, looking across the top of the table, he would locate the number "8" which represents the number of exemptions James Wray is claiming. The withholding tax is found at the intersection of the 610-620 line and column 8. The employer should withhold $76.00 from this paycheck.

When states and cities require an employer to withhold income taxes from their employees' paychecks, the tax calculations are handled much the same as with federal taxes.

Other Deductions

The deductions we have seen so far have been compulsory. In addition to these, the employee may authorize the employer to make deductions for union dues, insurance premiums, savings bonds, charitable contributions, or credit union deposits. In each situation, the amounts withheld must be forwarded to the proper agency.

EMPLOYER PAYROLL TAXES

Up to this point, we have discussed taxes that are withheld from the employee's paycheck. There are other payroll-related taxes levied directly on the employer. These taxes are based on the total earnings of the employees and may amount to a substantial business expense. Taxes which are levied directly on the employer are:

1. *FICA Tax.* As mentioned earlier, the employer must match the employee's contribution to Social Security.
2. *Federal Unemployment Compensation Tax.* Unemployment insurance is designed to provide financial relief to persons who have become unemployed because of economic conditions. The funds collected by the federal government are allocated to the states to help them administer their programs.
3. *State Unemployment Compensation Tax.* The funds received by the states from this tax are used to provide benefits to unemployed persons.

PAYROLL REGISTER

A payroll register is a specially designed form created to summarize the calculations used in preparing the payroll. An example of such a register is shown in Figure 12-2.

PAYROLL REGISTER

WEEK ENDED SEPT. 28, 19__

		DEDUCTIONS					DISTRIBUTION	
	GROSS PAY	FICA	INCOME TAXES	CREDIT UNION	NET PAY	CHECK NUMBER	OFFICE EXPENSE	SALES EXPENSE
Monica Brown	540.00	37.80	108.00	23.00	371.20	632	540.00	
Kevin Irwin	500.00	35.00	100.00	—	365.00	633		500.00
Martha Pagen	480.00	33.60	96.00	—	350.40	634		480.00
Chris Richards	400.00	28.00	80.00	15.00	277.00	635	400.00	
Yvonne Rivera	460.00	32.20	92.00	—	335.80	636	460.00	
Total	2,380.00	166.60	476.00	38.00	1,699.40		1,400.00	980.00

Figure 12-2. Payroll Register

Each line represents the pay calculations for one employee. Total deductions (FICA, income taxes, other deductions) are subtracted from the gross pay to arrive at net pay. The number of the check used to pay each employee is recorded in the Check Number column. The last two columns allocate the gross salary amounts between office salaries expense and sales salaries expense. The allocations are made according to the type of work performed by the employee.

Each column is totaled and these amounts are used to confirm that the individual employee calculations are correct. If the deduction totals are subtracted from the total gross pay, the difference should equal the total of the net pay column.

The payroll register is a flexible document which may be constructed to suit the needs of the company. It is not unusual for a payroll register to have additional columns for deductions or to give more detail on the calculation of gross pay.

RECORDING THE PAYROLL

Since the payroll register is a supplementary record, its information has not been recorded in the accounts. The journal entry to record the payroll shown in Figure 12-2 is:

Sept. 28	Office Salaries Expense	1400 —	
	Sales Salaries Expense	980 —	
	FICA Taxes Payable		166 60
	Employee Income Tax Payable		476 —
	Credit Union Deductions Payable		38 —
	Salaries Payable		1699 40

Note that the amounts recorded in the general journal entry are the column totals taken from the payroll register. The debits allocate the gross pay to the appropriate expense accounts, while the credits create current liabilities. All funds withheld from the payroll checks are payable to some private or governmental agency. The last credit is the total net pay owed to the employees. These liabilities are eliminated when payment is made to the respective parties.

RECORDING THE EMPLOYER'S TAXES

As previously discussed, there are taxes levied directly on the employer which must be recorded as an expense and a liability until paid. The entry to record the payroll tax expense and payroll tax liability is:

Sept. 28	Payroll Tax Expense	247 60	
	FICA Taxes Payable		166 60
	State Unemployment Taxes Payable		64 30
	Federal Unemployment Taxes Payable		16 70

Notice that the employer's FICA tax is equal to the total amount of FICA contributions withheld from the employees' paychecks. The FICA Taxes Payable account now has a balance of $333.20.

PROBLEMS

(Answers on page 114)

1. Patricia Lee earns $8 per hour for a standard 40-hour work week. Overtime pay is calculated using 150% of the regular hourly rate. Find her gross pay for a week in which she worked 45 hours.

2. Using the tax table provided on page 86, calculate the income tax withheld from the weekly paycheck of a married person who earns $447 and claims 4 exemptions.

3. The following information relates to the payroll for the week ending May 6.

Office salaries expense	$2,800
Sales salaries expense	4,200
FICA taxes withheld	490
Employee income taxes withheld	1,400
Medical insurance premiums withheld	210
Federal unemployment taxes	50
State unemployment taxes	140

a. Prepare the general journal entry to record the payroll.
b. Prepare the general journal entry to record the employer's payroll taxes.

13

THE WORKSHEET AND ADJUSTING ENTRIES

OBJECTIVES

After completing this chapter, you should be able to:

- Explain the purpose of a worksheet.
- Construct a worksheet.
- Prepare adjusting entries to correct year-end balances.

NEED FOR THE WORKSHEET

Way back in Chapter 1, we analyzed the steps involved in the accounting cycle. You should now refer to the illustrated accounting cycle (Figure 1-2) as we attempt to discover where we have been and where we are going.

Up to this point we have been in the recording phase of the cycle, since we have been interested solely in recording transactions in journals and posting the entries to the ledger accounts, and although we have discussed only three out of the ten steps, many of the remaining steps are short and fairly easy to perform.

Summarizing Phase

STEP	TASK
4	Accounts are balanced and the trial balance is prepared.
5	The worksheet is prepared.
6	Adjusting entries are journalized and posted.
7	Financial statements are prepared.
8	Financial statements are sent to management.
9	Closing entries are journalized and posted.
10	Post-closing trial balance is prepared.

The preparation of the worksheet is at the center of these activities. The summarizing phase occurs at the end of the accounting cycle and involves the manipulation of many details. The worksheet is prepared to reduce the likelihood of entering an error in the permanent records and to simplify the end-of-period procedures. This is not a formal statement and therefore is not given to management. It is normally prepared in pencil to make changes or corrections easy. After being prepared, the worksheet is used to create the financial statements and year-end journal entries.

CREATING THE UNADJUSTED TRIAL BALANCE

For the next two chapters, we will analyze the year-end procedures of a merchandising concern. As a starting point, we will assume that the bookkeepers at Tumelty Imports have accurately recorded and posted all transactions for the past year. Step 4 in the accounting cycle states that "accounts are balanced and the trial balance is prepared."

Tumelty Imports Unadjusted Trial Balance December 31, 19__	1	2
Cash	$ 7000—	
Accounts Receivable	10100—	
Allowance for Uncollectable Accounts		$ 100—
Merchandise Inventory	42000—	
Office Supplies	2000—	
Office Equipment	30000—	
Accumulated Depreciation—Office Equipment		3000—
Accounts Payable		5000—
John Tumelty, Capital		68000—
John Tumelty, Withdrawals	35000—	
Sales		305000—
Sales Returns and Allowances	5000—	
Purchases	182000—	
Purchase Returns and Allowances		2000—
Salaries Expense	50000—	
Rent Expense	7200—	
Advertising Expense	10000—	
Miscellaneous Expense	2800—	
	$383100—	$383100—

Note that the statement is labeled "*unadjusted* trial balance." This is due to the fact that some of the balances are incorrect and must be adjusted. The incorrect figures were not created by the bookkeepers. These are typical year-end activities needed to make the accounts current. The adjustments will be performed on the worksheet and then recorded in the journal and ledger.

ADJUSTING ENTRIES

Before we attempt to create a worksheet, we must adjust those accounts containing incorrect balances.

Adjustment A: A physical count of the office supplies shows that $1200 remain.

Analysis A: The unadjusted trial balance shows that the company has $2000 of office supplies. However, if a physical count reveals that only $1200 remains, then $1200 must be the correct balance. The company probably recorded all purchases of office supplies as debits to this account. During the same time, no entry was made to reduce the account balance when the office supplies were used. We know that when an asset is consumed, the asset account must be decreased with a credit and the expense account increased with a debit. The dollar value of this adjustment is the amount of supplies used.

$$
\begin{array}{rl}
\$2{,}000 & = \text{Account Balance} \\
-\,1{,}200 & = \text{Supplies on Hand} \\
\hline
\$\ \ 800 & = \text{Supplies Used}
\end{array}
$$

Adjusting Entry A:

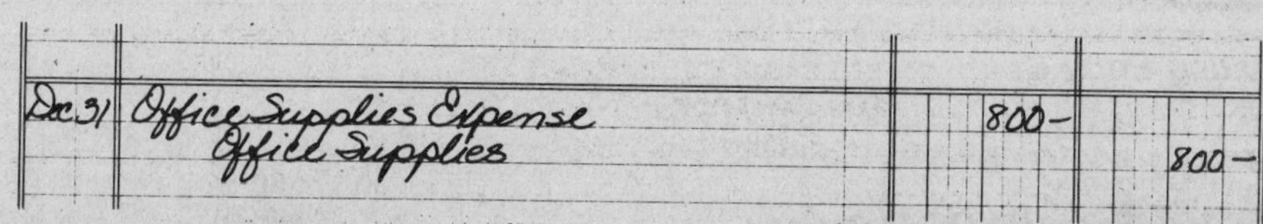

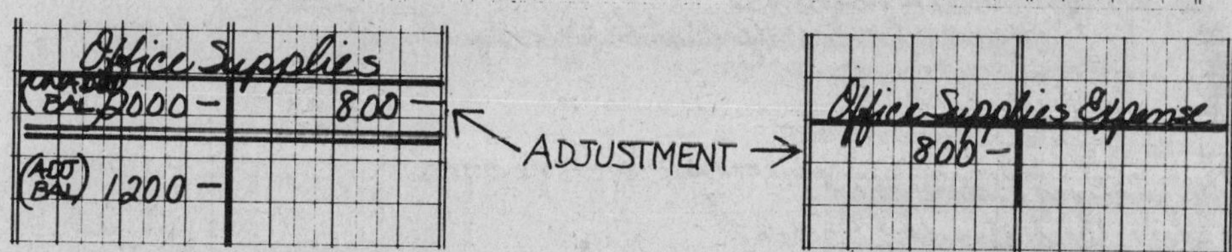

The asset account has a new balance of $1200 (down from $2000) and the expense account now has $800 recorded in it.

Adjustment B: It is estimated that uncollectable accounts are one-half of one percent of net credit sales of $300,000.

Analysis B: The first step in solving this problem is to calculate the estimated bad debts.

$$\$300{,}000 \times .005 = \$1500$$

From our previous work, we know that the entry calls for a debit to the expense account and a credit to the Allowance account.

Adjusting Entry B:

Date	Account	Debit	Credit
Dec. 31	Bad Debts Expense	1500—	
	Allowance for Uncollectable Accounts		1500—

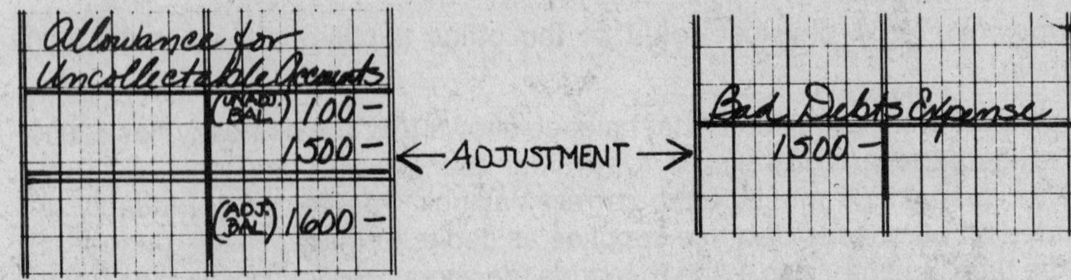

The Allowance account now has a $1600 credit balance and the expense account contains a $1500 credit balance.

Adjustment C: Estimated depreciation on the office equipment is 10% of cost.

Analysis C: The cost is the $30,000 debit balance in the Office Equipment account. Estimated depreciation for the past year is:

$$\$30,000 \times .10 = \$3,000$$

As discussed earlier, the entry to record the depreciation contains a debit to the Depreciation Expense account and a credit to the Accumulated Depreciation account.

Adjusting Entry C:

Date	Account	Debit	Credit
Dec. 31	Depreciation Expense	3000—	
	Accumulated Depreciation-Office Equipment		3000—

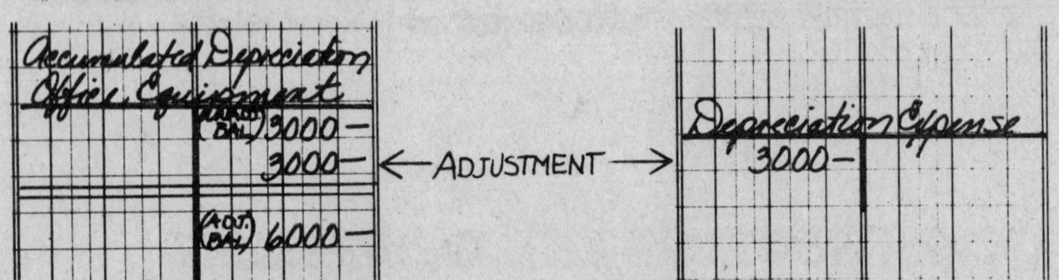

The Depreciation Expense account now contains a debit balance of $3000 and the Accumulated Depreciation balance has increased to $6000.

Adjustment D: Unrecorded salaries owed to employees amount to $500.

Analysis D: Since the last day of the accounting period usually does not coincide with a payroll payday, the company owes its employees wages for the time worked since the last payday. In this situation, the company owes the employees $500, which has not been included in salaries expense balance and has not been recognized as a liability.

Adjusting Entry D:

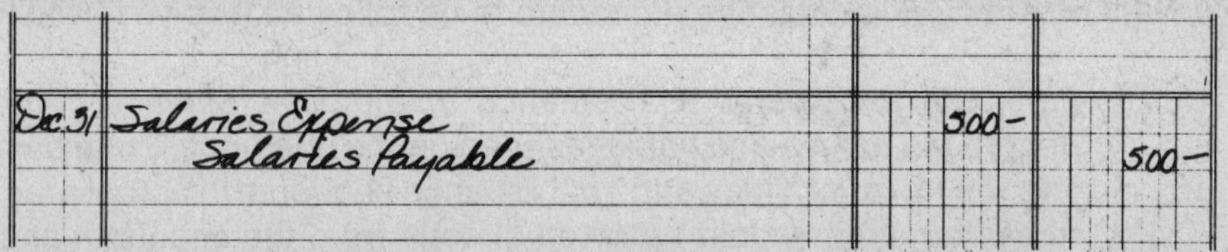

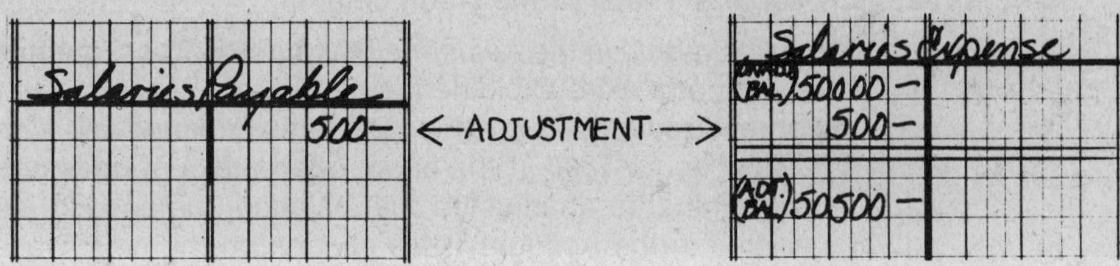

The balance sheet will now show that the company has a $500 liability to its employees, and the full amount of the company's salaries expense ($50,500) will be recorded on the income statement.

Adjustment E: The merchandise inventory balance on December 31 is $40,000.

Analysis E: The merchandise inventory balance on the unadjusted trial balance ($42,000) represents the value of the inventory at the beginning of the year. By the end of the year, the balance had changed to $40,000, which means that the merchandise inventory balance must be changed. This change will be made in closing entries to be prepared later. In the closing entries, we will credit the Merchandise Inventory account for $42,000 to remove the old inventory and debit the account for $40,000 to show the new balance.

CONSTRUCTING THE WORKSHEET

The worksheet contains 5 pairs of columns, or 10 columns in all. The 5 sections are:

1. Trial Balance (Unadjusted)
2. Adjustments
3. Adjusted Trial Balance
4. Income Statement
5. Balance Sheet

We will study the construction of the worksheet by referring to the Tumelty Imports worksheet. The procedure to be followed involves five steps.

1. *Enter the unadjusted trial balance in the Trial Balance columns.* Record the names and balances seen on the unadjusted trial balance into the Account Titles and Trial Balance sections. In actual practice, this information would be taken directly from the accounts and not from a prepared trial balance. The total of the debit column must naturally equal the total of the credit column.
2. *Enter the adjustments in the Adjustments columns.* The adjustments for Tumelty Imports were explained earlier in this chapter. The first adjustment required a debit to Office Supplies Expense and a credit to Office Supplies for $800. If the name of an account does not appear on the original or unadjusted trial balance, the account name must be written in the Account Titles section on the next available line. This is the situation with Office Supplies Expense. The debit to this account is recorded in the Debit column of the Adjustments section and is keyed with a letter for easy identification. Since the Office Supplies account appeared on the original trial balance, the credit can be entered opposite the account name in the Credit column of the Adjustments section. Notice that it is keyed with the same letter as its related debit. After all adjustments have been recorded in the same manner, the columns are totaled (of course, the debits must equal the credits). Note also that the last adjusting entry (merchandise inventory) was not recorded in this section. It will be recorded later in the Income Statement and Balance Sheet sections.
3. *Adjust the balances, and record in the Adjusted Trial Balance columns.* The balances from the first two sections must now be brought over to the Adjusted Trial Balance columns. If the account was not adjusted, the balance can be brought directly into its corresponding column. For example, the cash balance received no adjustment and, therefore, the $7000 debit balance should be brought over to the Debit column of the Adjusted Trial Balance.

   When an account has been adjusted, it is necessary to add to or subtract from the unadjusted balance. If the unadjusted amount is a debit and the adjustment is a debit, the two amounts are added to create a larger debit. Two credits are similarly added to produce a larger credit. (See Salaries Expense and Allowance for Uncollectable Accounts.) When the two balances are not alike, the smaller balance is subtracted from the larger and the resulting balance has the same designation as the larger balance. Notice office supplies:

$2,000	(DR) Unadjusted Balance
−800	(CR) Adjustment
1,200	(DR) Adjusted Balance

   Finally, if a new account was created, consider it to have a zero beginning balance and just bring over the debit or credit from the Adjustments section. (See Office Supplies Expense.)

_______________ ◄Name

Tumelty Imports
Work Sheet
For the Year Ending December 31, 19__

Account Name	Trial Balance		Adjustments		Adjusted Trial Balance		Income Statement		Balance Sheet	
	Debit	Credit	Debit	Credit	Debit	Credit	Debit	Credit	Debit	Credit
Cash	7000 –				7000 –				7000 –	
Accounts Receivable	10100 –				10100 –				10100 –	
Allowance for Uncol. Accounts		100 –		(b) 1500 –		1600 –				1600 –
Merchandise Inventory	42000 –				42000 –		(e) 42000 –	(e) 40000 –	40000 –	
Office Supplies	2000 –			(a) 800 –	1200 –				1200 –	
Office Equipment	30000 –				30000 –				30000 –	
Accumulated Deprec. - Office Eq.		3000 –		(c) 3000 –		6000 –				6000 –
Accounts Payable		5000 –				5000 –				5000 –
John Tumelty, Capital		68000 –				68000 –				68000 –
John Tumelty, Withdrawals	35000 –				35000 –				35000 –	
Sales		305000 –				305000 –		305000 –		
Sales Returns and Allowances	5000 –				5000 –		5000 –			
Purchases	182000 –				182000 –		182000 –			
Purchase Returns and Allowances		2000 –				2000 –		2000 –		
Salaries Expense	50000 –		(d) 500 –		50500 –		50500 –			
Rent Expense	7200 –				7200 –		7200 –			
Advertising Expense	10000 –				10000 –		10000 –			
Miscellaneous Expense	2800 –				2800 –		2800 –			
	383100 –	383100 –								
Office Supplies Expense			(a) 800 –		800 –		800 –			
Bad Debts Expense			(b) 1500 –		1500 –		1500 –			
Depreciation Expense-Office Eq.			(c) 3000 –		3000 –		3000 –			
Salaries Payable				(d) 500 –		500 –				500 –
			5800 –	5800 –	388100 –	388100 –	304800 –	347000 –	123300 –	81100 –
							42200 –			42200 –
							347000 –	347000 –	123300 –	123300 –

The Adjusted Trial Balance columns are added and the equality of debits and credits must be maintained.

4. *Extend the balances in the Adjusted Trial Balance columns into the Income Statement and Balance Sheet sections.* For each account, determine the financial statement it would appear on and move the balance over from the Adjusted Trial Balance section to that financial statement section. Assets, liabilities, capital and withdrawal accounts are brought over to the Balance Sheet section. Revenue and expense accounts are brought over to the Income Statement section. It is important to maintain the same debit or credit account balance that existed in the adjusted trial balance.

   There was one adjustment which was not recorded in the Adjustments section. The *old* Merchandise Inventory account balance ($42,000) should now be brought over to the debit column of the Income Statement and the *new* balance ($40,000) should be entered in *both* the credit column of the Income Statement section *and* the debit column of the Balance Sheet section. The reason for the dual entry in the Income Statement section is because the fluctuation in inventory has an impact on the net income of the firm. This can be seen in the Cost of Goods Sold section of the income statement, where Merchandise Inventory appears two times. The debit of $40,000 in the Balance Sheet section shows that the current value of the inventory is recorded in the balance sheet.

5. *Total all columns in the Income Statement and Balance Sheet sections and calculate the net income or net loss.* After all columns are totaled, the two Income Statement columns will probably not be equal. The same is true of the Balance Sheet columns. Find the difference between the two Income Statement columns, which will represent either the net profit or net loss for the company. If the credits are larger than the debits, the difference is a credit and represents the net income. If the difference has a debit balance, it shows a net loss from operations. In this problem, the difference between the Income Statement columns is $42,200. Since this represents an excess of credits over debits, we know the company made a $42,200 net profit.

   But now to confirm this balance. If we add this amount to the smaller balance in *both* the Income Statement and Balance Sheet sections, it should cause both sets of columns to balance. It is easy to understand why the Income Statement columns balance. After all, we subtracted the debit column from the credit column to arrive at the $42,200 amount, so it should balance when added back again. But can you tell why the addition of this profit causes the Balance Sheet columns to balance?

   The reason is that, until this point, we were using the owner's old capital, which does not reflect the fact that he earned a profit in the past year. A profit naturally increases the owner's capital, and withdrawals decrease the balance. The withdrawals were there, but not the profit.

   When the net income or net loss is added in each section, each set of columns should balance.

PROBLEMS

(Answers on page 115)

1. The following account titles have balances in the Adjusted Trial Balance section of the worksheet. For each account, identify the section its balance would be extended to (Income Statement or Balance Sheet) and indicate whether it would be recorded in the debit or credit column.

ACCOUNT	STATEMENT		BALANCE	
	INCOME STATEMENT	BALANCE SHEET	DEBIT	CREDIT
Cash (example)		X	X	
Sales				
Rent Expense				
Accounts Receivable				
Allowance for Uncollectable Accounts				
Purchases				
Salaries Payable				
Suzanne Lynn, Capital				
Bad Debts Expense				
Suzanne Lynn, Withdrawals				

2. Create general journal entries to record the following year-end adjustments.

- **a.** The Store Supplies account had a debit balance of $1500, but a physical inventory showed $1000 of supplies on hand.
- **b.** Estimated bad debt losses are estimated to be one-half of 1% of the $200,000 credit sales.
- **c.** Estimated depreciation on the store equipment is estimated at $725.
- **d.** Salaries owed to employees at year-end amount to $980.

14

CLOSING THE BOOKS

OBJECTIVES

After completing this chapter, you should be able to:

- Prepare an income statement, statement of retained earnings, and balance sheet from the information contained on the worksheet.
- Prepare adjusting and closing entries from the worksheet.
- Explain why closing entries are needed at the end of the accounting cycle.
- Create a post-closing trial balance and explain why it is used.

JOURNALIZE AND POST ADJUSTING ENTRIES

In this chapter, we will see how valuable the worksheet is in completing the year-end activities. The remaining activities in the accounting cycle (Steps 6–10) can be performed using the information developed on the worksheet.

Although the last chapter showed the general journal entry for each adjustment, this was only for instructional purposes. The recording of the adjusting entries would normally wait until the worksheet was complete. At that time, one would only have to look in the Adjustments section to find the keyed debits and credits for each entry. A brief look at the two columns reveals that transaction (a) had an $800 debit to Office Supplies expense and a credit to Office Supplies. This entry can now be recorded in the general journal and posted to the individual accounts. The general journal entries taken from the worksheet are:

	Adjusting Entries		
Dec. 31	Office Supplies Expense	800 –	
	Office Supplies		800 –
31	Bad Debts Expense	1500 –	
	Allowance for Uncollectable Accounts		1500 –
31	Depreciation Expense	3000 –	
	Accumulated Depreciation-Office Eq.		3000 –
31	Salaries Expense	500 –	
	Salaries Payable		500 –

When posted, these entries correct the balances in the affected accounts. Note the last adjustment, (e), was not recorded at this time. It will be included in the closing entries, which are to come.

FINANCIAL STATEMENT PREPARATION

All the data necessary to create the financial statements are in the Income Statement and Balance Sheet sections. There are three financial statements to be prepared and, logically, they must be prepared in the following sequence:

1. Income Statement
2. Statement of Owner's Equity
3. Balance Sheet

Earlier, we analyzed the structure of the income statement for a merchandising concern. The following is the income statement for Tumelty Imports, prepared from the Income Statement section of the worksheet.

Tumelty Imports
Income Statement
For the Year Ending December 31, 19__

	1	2	3	4
Revenue:				
Gross Sales				# 305000 —
Less: Sales Returns and Allowances				− 5000 —
Net Sales				# 300000 —
Cost of Goods Sold:				
Merchandise Inventory Jan 1, 19__			# 42000 —	
Purchases		# 182000 —		
Less: Purchase Returns and Allowances		2000 —		
Cost of Goods Purchased			180000 —	
Cost of Goods Available for Sale			# 222000 —	
Less: Merchandise Inventory Dec 31, 19__			40000 —	
Cost of Goods Sold				182000 —
Gross Profit on Sales				# 118000 —
Operating Expenses:				
Salaries Expense			# 50500 —	
Rent Expense			7200 —	
Advertising Expense			10000 —	
Miscellaneous Expense			2800 —	
Office Supplies Expense			800 —	
Bad Debts Expense			1500 —	
Depreciation Expense			3000 —	
Total Operating Expenses				75800 —
Net Income				# 42200 —

The net income derived in the formal report must naturally agree with the net income calculated on the worksheet.

The second report to be prepared is the statement of owner's equity, which could not have been created prior to the calculation of the net income or net loss. The statement of owner's equity shows how the owner's capital has changed from the beginning to the end of the accounting period. When the business records a net income for the period, the owner's capital is increased by the amount of the profit. Withdrawals made by the owner and net losses decrease the capital. The statement of owner's equity for Tumelty Imports follows:

Tumelty Imports Statement of Owner's Equity December 31, 19__	1	2
John Tumelty, Capital Jan 1, 19__		$ 68000 —
ADD: Net Income for 19__		42200 —
Subtotal		$ 110200 —
LESS: Withdrawals for 19__		35000 —
John Tumelty, Capital, Dec. 31, 19__		$ 75200 —

The owner's ending capital balance can now be used in the Owner's Equity section of the balance sheet.

The structure of the balance sheet has not changed much since the early chapters. Assets still must equal liabilities plus owner's equity. Assets have been divided into two types:

Current Assets — Those assets which will be consumed within one year.

Plant and Equipment — Assets which have a life expectancy greater than one year.

Liabilities are also divided into two categories. Current liabilities are those debts which must be paid within one year. If the time period is greater than one year, the obligation is considered to be a long-term liability.

The balance sheet on page 103 for Tumelty Imports was taken from the Balance Sheet section of the worksheet. The only exception is the capital balance, which was brought over from the statement of owner's equity.

Once the financial statements have been prepared, they can be forwarded to management and other interested parties.

JOURNALIZE AND POST CLOSING ENTRIES

At the end of the accounting period, there are certain account balances which should not be brought over into the next period. In the Tumelty Imports

Tumelty Imports
Balance Sheet
December 31, 19—

	1	2	3
Assets			
Current Assets:			
Cash		$ 7000—	
Accounts Receivable	$ 10100—		
Allowance for Uncollectable Accounts	1600—	8500—	
Merchandise Inventory		40000—	
Office Supplies		1200—	
Total Current Assets			$ 56700—
Plant and Equipment:			
Office Equipment		$ 30000—	
Less: Accumulated Depreciation		6000—	
Total Plant and Equipment			24000—
Total Assets			$ 80700—
Liabilities			
Current Liabilities:			
Accounts Payable		$ 5000—	
Salaries Payable		500—	
Total Current Liabilities			$ 5500—
Owner's Equity			
John Tumelty, Capital			75200—
Total Liabilities and Owner's Equity			$ 80700

problem, the Salaries Expense account has a debit balance of $50,500 and the Sales account has a credit balance of $305,000.

Salaries Expense	
50500—	

Sales	
	305000—

If nothing is done with these balances, they will remain in the accounts and next year's salaries expense and sales figures will be added on top of the left-over amounts. These accounts, among others, must be closed out or brought down to a zero balance. In fact, every account in the Income Statement section of the worksheet as well as the Withdrawals account in the Balance Sheet section must start the new year with a zero balance.

A second problem we have to resolve relates to the balance in the Capital account, which currently is $68,000. This balance must be increased by the amount of the net income and decreased by the amount of the withdrawals.

Both of these objectives can be accomplished through the use of closing entries, which are prepared using the following procedures:

1. *Every account with debit balance in the Income Statement section of the worksheet is closed out to the Income Summary account.* If an account has a debit balance, it can be brought down to a zero balance by crediting it for the amount of its balance. This accounts for the large number of credits in the first entry. The only debit will be to a new account called Income Summary. After the second closing entry, this account will have a balance representing the net income of the company. The first closing entry for Tumelty Imports is:

		1	2
Dec. 31	Income Summary	304800 —	
	Merchandise Inventory		42000 —
	Sales Returns and Allowances		5000 —
	Purchases		182000 —
	Salaries Expense		50500 —
	Rent Expense		7200 —
	Advertising Expense		10000 —
	Miscellaneous Expense		2800 —
	Office Supplies Expense		800 —
	Bad Debts Expense		1500 —
	Depreciation Expense - Office Eq.		3000 —

2. *Every account with a credit balance in the Income Statement section of the worksheet is closed out to the Income Summary account.* The debits to these accounts will bring their balances to zero. After the Income Summary account has received the credit from this transaction, its balance represents the net income of the firm.

Dec. 31	Merchandise Inventory	40000 —	
	Sales	305000 —	
	Purchase Returns and Allowances	2000 —	
	Income Summary		347000 —

	Income Summary		
(Closing entry 1)	304800 —	347000 —	(Closing entry 2)
		42200 —	(Net Income)

3. *Close the balance in the Income Summary account to the Capital account.* This entry increases the owner's capital by the amount of the net income.

Date	Account	Debit	Credit
Dec. 31	Income Summary	42200—	
	John Tumelty, Capital		42200—

John Tumelty, Capital

Debit	Credit
	68000— (Jan 1)
	42200— (Net Income)

Income Summary

Debit	Credit
42200—	42200— (Net Income)

CLOSING ENTRY

4. *Close the balance in the Withdrawals account to the Capital account.* This entry reduces the owner's capital by the amount of withdrawals made during the year. It also brings the Withdrawals account balance down to zero to start the new year.

Date	Account	Debit	Credit
Dec. 31	John Tumelty, Capital	35000—	
	John Tumelty, Withdrawals		35000—

John Tumelty, Withdrawals

Debit	Credit
(Bal.) 35000—	35000—

John Tumelty, Capital

Debit	Credit
35000—	68000— (Jan 1)
	42200— (Net Income)
35000—	110200—
	75200— (Dec 31, Bal.)

CLOSING ENTRY

Note that the new balance in the Capital account ($75,200) is the same amount calculated in the statement of owner's equity.

PREPARE THE POST-CLOSING TRIAL BALANCE

The final step in the accounting cycle is the preparation of a post-closing trial balance. At this point, many of the accounts have been closed and therefore have zero balances. Only the asset, liability, and capital accounts remain open. Because all adjusting and closing entries have been recorded and posted, the remaining accounts should have correct balances in them. To be sure, we must prepare a post-closing trial balance. This statement uses only those accounts which continue to have balances. The Tumelty Imports post-closing trial balance is:

Tumelty Imports
Post-Closing Trial Balance
December 31, 19__

Account	1	2
Cash	$ 7000 –	
Accounts Receivable	10100 –	
Allowance for Uncollectable Accounts		1600 –
Merchandise Inventory	40000 –	
Office Supplies	1200 –	
Office Equipment	30000 –	
Accumulated Depreciation-Office Eq.		6000 –
Accounts Payable		5000 –
Salaries Payable		500 –
John Tumelty, Capital		75200 –
	88300 –	88300 –

PROBLEMS

(Answers on page 115)

1. Jane Warren, a lawyer, has the following year-end balances in selected accounts:

Jane Warren, Capital

	60,000 (Bal.)

Salaries Expense

(Bal.) 15,000	

Jane Warren, Withdrawals

(Bal.) 20,000	

Rent Expense

(Bal.) 10,000	

Income Summary

Office Supplies Expense

(Bal.) 2,000	

Legal Fees Earned

	50,000 (Bal.)

Insurance Expense

(Bal.) 1,000	

a. Prepare journal entries to close the accounts.
b. Post the journal entries to the T accounts.

2. Using the data provided in the previous problem, create a statement of owner's equity for Jane Warren.

ANSWERS TO CHAPTER PROBLEMS

CHAPTER 2

1. ASSETS = LIABILITIES + OWNER'S EQUITY

2. The left side shows what the firm owns and the right side tells who provided the financial resources to purchase the assets. Therefore, a company cannot have more or less assets than financial resources provided.

3.

Account Name	Financial Statement	Section
Legal Fees Earned	Income Statement	Revenue
Notes Payable	Balance Sheet	Liabilities
Accounts Recelvable	Balance Sheet	Assets
Office Supplies	Balance Sheet	Assets
Rent Expense	Income Statement	Expenses
Richard Lent, Capital	Balance Sheet	Owner's Equity
Office Supplies Expense	Income Statement	Expenses

4.

	ASSETS				= LIABILITIES	+ OWNER'S EQUITY
	Cash	Office Supplies	Furniture	Office Equipment	Accounts Payable	R. Lent, Capital
(a)	$10,000					$10,000
(b)	− 600		+600			
Bal.	$ 9,400		$600			$10,000
(c)		+$200		+$1,000	+1,200	
Bal.	$ 9,400	$200	$600	$1,000	$1,200	$10,000
(d)	− 1,200				−1,200	
Bal.	$ 8,200	$200	$600	$1,000	0	$10,000

CHAPTER 3

1.

ACCOUNT	TYPE OF ACCOUNT	INCREASE	DECREASE	NORMAL BALANCE
Cash	ASSET	DEBIT	CREDIT	DEBIT
Accounts Payable	LIABILITY	CREDIT	DEBIT	CREDIT
Interest Expense	EXPENSE	DEBIT	CREDIT	DEBIT
William Hynes, Withdrawals	OWNER'S EQUITY	DEBIT	CREDIT	DEBIT
Accounts Receivable	ASSET	DEBIT	CREDIT	DEBIT
Rental Fees Earned	REVENUE	CREDIT	DEBIT	CREDIT
Unearned Fees	LIABILITY	CREDIT	DEBIT	CREDIT
William Hynes, Capital	OWNER'S EQUITY	CREDIT	DEBIT	CREDIT

2.

Cash

(a) 10,000	75 (c)
(d) 2,000	125 (e)
(i) 1,500	600 (g)
	120 (h)
	2,000 (j)
	480 (k)
13,500	3,400
(Bal.) 10,100	

R. Augustine, Capital

	10,000 (a)

R. Augustine, Withdrawals

(g) 600	

Commissions Earned

	2,000 (d)
	3,500 (f)
	5,500 (Bal.)

Accounts Receivable

(f) 3,500	1,500 (i)
(Bal.) 2,000	

Office Equipment

(b) 4,400	

Advertising Expense

(e) 125	

Accounts Payable

(j) 2,000	4,400 (b)
	2,400 (Bal.)

Rent Expense

(k) 480	

Utilities Expense

(h) 120	

Office Supplies

(c) 75	

CHAPTER 4

1.

Date		Account	Debit	Credit
June	1	Cash	5,000	
		Mary Reynolds, Capital		5,000
	4	Medical Supplies	800	
		Cash		800
	7	Medical Equipment	1,200	
		Cash		500
		Accounts Payable		700
	12	Cash	250	
		Veterinary Fees		250
	16	Medical Supplies	80	
		Accounts Payable		80
	21	Accounts Receivable	400	
		Veterinary Fees		400
	23	Accounts Payable	80	
		Cash		80
	28	Cash	200	
		Accounts Receivable		200
	30	Utilities Expense	100	
		Cash		100

2.

Cash

Debit	Credit
(6/1) 5,000	800 (6/4)
(6/12) 250	500 (6/7)
(6/28) 200	80 (6/23)
	100 (6/30)

Accounts Payable

Debit	Credit
(6/23) 80	700 (6/7)
	80 (6/16)

Mary Reynolds, Capital

Debit	Credit
	5,000 (6/1)

Accounts Receivable

Debit	Credit
(6/21) 400	200 (6/28)

Veterinary Fees

Debit	Credit
	250 (6/12)
	400 (6/21)

Medical Supplies

Debit	Credit
(6/4) 800	
(6/16) 80	

Medical Equipment

Debit	Credit
(6/7) 1,200	

Utilities Expense

Debit	Credit
(6/30) 100	

3.

Mary Reynolds D.V.M.
Trial Balance
Dec. 31, 19__

Cash	$3,970	
Accounts Receivable	200	
Medical Supplies	880	
Medical Equipment	1,200	
Accounts Payable		$ 700
Veterinary Fees		650
Utilities Expense	100	
Mary Reynolds, Capital		5,000
	$6,350	$6,350

CHAPTER 5

1.

April	8	Accounts Receivable	2,000	
		Sales		2,000
	10	Sales Returns and Allowances	200	
		Accounts Receivable		200
	13	Accounts Receivable	1,000	
		Sales		1,000
	18	Cash	1,764	
		Sales Discounts	36	
		Accounts Receivable		1,800
	24	Cash	80	
		Sales		80
	30	Cash	1,000	
		Accounts Receivable		1,000

2.

Aug.	1	Purchases	1,100	
		Accounts Payable		1,100
	3	Accounts Payable	100	
		Purchase Returns and Allowances		100
	7	Purchases	160	
		Cash		160
	9	Purchases	1,800	
		Accounts Payable		1,800
	11	Accounts Payable	1,000	
		Purchase Discounts		20
		Cash		980
	31	Accounts Payable	1,800	
		Cash		1,800

CHAPTER 6

1.

a. Sales
b. Cash Payments
c. Cash Receipts
d. Purchases
e. General Journal
f. Cash Receipts
g. Cash Payments
h. Cash Payments

2.

a. General Journal
b. Accounts Receivable – Debit
Sales – Credit
c. Purchases – Debit
Accounts Payable – Credit
d. Accounts Receivable Ledger
Accounts Payable Ledger

CHAPTER 7

1.

A B C

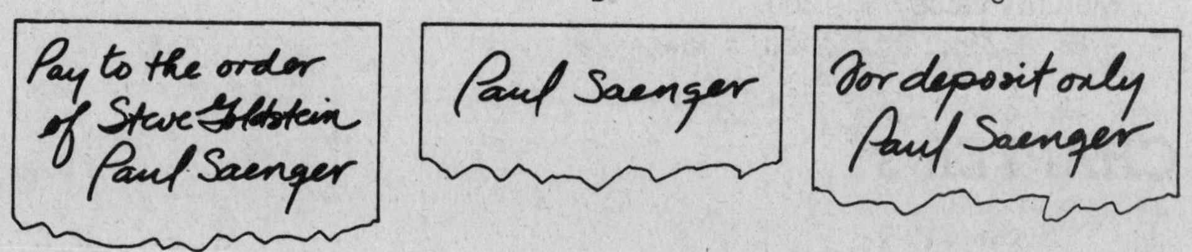

A. Full Endorsement **B.** Blank Endorsement **C.** Restrictive Endorsement

2A.

Connamara Marble Co.
Bank Reconciliation
October 15, 19__

Book balance	$2,048	Bank balance	$3,520
ADD:		ADD:	
Proceeds of note	1,300	Deposit in transit	430
	$3,348		$3,950
DEDUCT:		DEDUCT:	
Service charge	18	Outstanding checks	620
Corrected balance	$3,330	Corrected balance	$3,330

B.

Oct.	15	Cash	1,300	
		Notes Receivable		1,300
	15	Miscellaneous Expense	18	
		Cash		18

c. $3,330

3.

			Debit	Credit
Feb.	2	Petty Cash	100	
		Cash		100
March	5	Office Supplies	27	
		Delivery Expense	31	
		Transportation Expense	19	
		Miscellaneous Expense	6	
		Cash		83
March	5	Petty Cash	50	
		Cash		50

CHAPTER 8

1.

a. Wallace Lumber Co.
b. Charles and Carol Calhoun
c. May 19
d. August 17
e. $10,000
f. 12%
g. 90 days

2. Interest = $300
Maturity value = $10,300

CHAPTER 9

1.

			Debit	Credit
June	8	Purchases	7,000	
		Notes Payable		7,000
	11	Cash	9,850	
		Interest Expense	150	
		Notes Payable		10,000
	17	Accounts Payable – Spellman Co.	2,000	
		Notes Payable		2,000
July	8	Notes Payable	7,000	
		Interest Expense	70	
		Cash		7,070
	26	Notes Payable	10,000	
		Cash		10,000
Aug.	16	Notes Payable	2,000	
		Interest Expense	50	
		Cash		2,050

2.

Arnaiz Co.

			Debit	Credit
June	8	Notes Receivable	7,000	
		Sales		7,000

Bank of Southport

June 11	Notes Receivable	10,000	
	Interest Income		150
	Cash		9,850

Spellman Co.

June 17	Notes Receivable	2,000	
	Accounts Receivable—Drummond Co.		2,000

Arnaiz Co.

July 8	Cash	7,070	
	Interest Income		70
	Notes Receivable		7,000

Bank of Southport

July 26	Cash	10,000	
	Notes Receivable		10,000

Spellman Co.

Aug. 16	Cash	2,050	
	Interest Income		50
	Notes Receivable		2,000

CHAPTER 10

1.

a. $2080

$$I = \frac{2000}{1} \times \frac{16}{100} \times \frac{90}{360}$$

$$I = \$80$$

$$MV = \$2000 + \$80$$
$$MV = \$2080$$

b. $2054

$$CP = \$2080 - \left(\frac{2080}{1} \times \frac{15}{100} \times \frac{30}{360}\right)$$

$$CP = 2080 - 26$$
$$CP = \$2054$$

c. $54

2.

a. April	20	Notes Receivable	2,000	
		Accounts Receivable—Mary Green		2,000
b. June	19	Cash	2,054	
		Interest Income		54
		Notes Receivable Discounted		2,000

c. July	19	Notes Receivable Discounted	2,000	
		Notes Receivable		2,000
	19	Accounts Receivable—Mary Green	2,080	
		Cash		2,080
d. Aug.	18	Cash	2,107.73	
		Accounts Receivable—Mary Green		2,080
		Interest Income		27.73

CHAPTER 11

1.

a. June	14	Bad Debts Expense	1,100	
		Accounts Receivable—Raleigh		1,100
b. Nov.	17	Accounts Receivable—Raleigh	1,100	
		Bad Debts Expense		1,100

2.

a. Dec.	31	Bad Debts Expense	2,500	
		Allowance for Uncollectable Accounts		2,500
b. Jan.	21	Allowance for Uncollectable Accounts	400	
		Accounts Receivable—F. Farbent		400
c. May	19	Accounts Receivable—F. Farbent	400	
		Allowance for Uncollectable Accounts		400
	19	Cash	400	
		Accounts Receivable—F. Farbent		400

CHAPTER 12

1. $380

   GP = (40 × $8) + 1.5(8) (45 − 40)
   GP = 320 + 60
   GP = 380

2. $53.40

3.

a. May	6	Office Salaries Expense	2,800	
		Sales Salaries Expense	4,200	
		FICA Taxes Payable		490
		Income Taxes Payable		1,400
		Medical Premiums Payable		210
		Salaries Payable		4,900
b. May	6	Payroll Tax Expense	680	
		FICA Taxes Payable		490
		Federal Unemployment Taxes Payable		50
		State Unemployment Taxes Payable		140

CHAPTER 13

1.

ACCOUNT	STATEMENT		BALANCE	
	INCOME STATEMENT	BALANCE SHEET	DEBIT	CREDIT
Cash		X	X	
Sales	X			X
Rent Expense	X		X	
Accounts Receivable		X	X	
Allowance for Uncollectable Accounts		X		X
Purchases	X		X	
Salaries Payable		X		X
Suzanne Lynn, Capital		X		X
Bad Debts Expense	X		X	
Suzanne Lynn, Withdrawals		X	X	

2.

a.	Dec. 31	Store Supplies Expense	500	
		Store Supplies		500
b.	Dec. 31	Bad Debts Expense	1,000	
		Allowance for Uncollectable Accounts		1,000
c.	Dec. 31	Depreciation Expense	725	
		Accumulated Depreciation —Store Equipment		725
d.	Dec. 31	Salaries Expense	980	
		Salaries Payable		980

CHAPTER 14

1.

Dec. 31	Income Summary	28,000	
	Salaries Expense		15,000
	Rent Expense		10,000
	Office Supplies Expense		2,000
	Insurance Expense		1,000
Dec. 31	Legal Fees Earned	50,000	
	Income Summary		50,000
Dec. 31	Income Summary	22,000	
	Jane Warren, Capital		22,000
Dec. 31	Jane Warren, Capital	20,000	
	Jane Warren, Withdrawals		20,000

b.

Jane Warren, Capital	
Withdrawals 20,000	60,000 (Bal.)
	22,000 (Net Income)
20,000	82,000
	62,000 (Ending Bal.)

Jane Warren, Withdrawals	
(Bal.) 20,000	20,000 (Dec. 31)

Income Summary	
(Dec. 31) 28,000	50,000 (Dec. 31)
(Dec. 31) 22,000	22,000 (Net Income)

Legal Fees Earned	
(Dec. 31) 50,000	50,000 (Bal.)

Salaries Expense	
(Bal.) 15,000	15,000 (Dec. 31)

Rent Expense	
(Bal.) 10,000	10,000 (Dec. 31)

Office Supplies Expense	
(Bal.) 2,000	2,000 (Dec. 31)

Insurance Expense	
(Bal.) 1,000	1,000 (Dec. 31)

2.

Jane Warren
Statement of Owner's Equity
December 31, 19__

Jane Warren, Capital, Jan. 1, 19__	$60,000
ADD: Net Income for 19__	22,000
Subtotal	$82,000
LESS: Withdrawals for 19__	20,000
Jane Warren, Capital, Dec. 31, 19__	$62,000

INDEX